CUBA: ASSESSING THE ADMINISTRATION'S SUDDEN SHIFT

HEARING

BEFORE THE

COMMITTEE ON FOREIGN AFFAIRS HOUSE OF REPRESENTATIVES

ONE HUNDRED FOURTEENTH CONGRESS

FIRST SESSION

FEBRUARY 4, 2015

Serial No. 114–15

Printed for the use of the Committee on Foreign Affairs

Available via the World Wide Web: http://www.foreignaffairs.house.gov/ or http://www.gpo.gov/fdsys/

U.S. GOVERNMENT PUBLISHING OFFICE

93–157PDF   WASHINGTON : 2015

For sale by the Superintendent of Documents, U.S. Government Publishing Office
Internet: bookstore.gpo.gov   Phone: toll free (866) 512–1800; DC area (202) 512–1800
Fax: (202) 512–2104   Mail: Stop IDCC, Washington, DC 20402–0001

CONTENTS

CUBA: ASSESSING THE ADMINISTRATION'S SUDDEN SHIFT

WEDNESDAY, FEBRUARY 4, 2015

HOUSE OF REPRESENTATIVES,
COMMITTEE ON FOREIGN AFFAIRS,
Washington, DC.

The committee met, pursuant to notice, at 10:08 a.m., in room 2172, Rayburn House Office Building, Hon. Ed Royce (chairman of the committee) presiding.

Chairman ROYCE. This hearing will come to order.

Today we look at the Obama administration's sudden shift on Cuba policy. And sudden it was. Members of Congress were left in the dark. Most of the administration—including the State Department—was left in the dark. Instead, talks with the Cuban regime were conducted by two White House officials. Unfortunately the White House was unwilling to provide these key witnesses today. This committee, charged with oversight of our foreign policy, is handicapped when those officials most involved in policy making are unavailable. The administration's growing track record of secret negotiations, whether this is on the subject of Iran or the release of the five Taliban commanders, is increasingly troublesome.

Had the White House consulted more widely, it may have heard that Havana is facing the threats of losing Venezuelan oil subsidies and mounting public pressure for basic reforms within the country. This could have been used to leverage meaningful political concessions on human rights in Cuba by that regime. But this was a one-sided "negotiation," with the U.S. making a series of concessions to Havana.

The release of 53 political prisoners is one area in which the administration did secure a commitment from the Cuban Government. But in an odd twist, the administration kept these names secret for weeks. Only after bipartisan pressure from the committee was the list ever released, and human rights advocates can now track whether these individuals are put back in jail, harassed, or monitored.

Of course, 4 years ago, Raul Castro promised to release all political prisoners. Yet in a recent Freedom House report, we read that: "Systematic use of short-term 'preventable' detentions—along with harassment [and] beatings," are used to intimidate the opposition, to isolate dissidents, and maintain control. Advocates put the number of political arrests in Cuba last year at over 8,000.

Assistant Secretary Jacobson, I appreciate very much your meeting with dissidents while you were in Havana last month. But I am very concerned that your Cuban counterparts are attempting to link your discussions to a commitment that the U.S. cease all democracy programs.

Indeed, Castro is making even more demands. Last week, the dictator called for the return of the U.S. Naval station, an end to U.S. broadcasts, and ''just compensation,'' in his words. There is little debate over the importance of this facility for the U.S. Navy to conduct counternarcotics, intelligence, and humanitarian missions. And of course, our broadcasts are vital until a free media is allowed to operate. I hope the State Department is here today to assure us that none of Castro's demands are being considered.

In defending this policy change, the President has compared our economic relationship with Cuba to that of China and Vietnam. But in China and in Vietnam, while Communist, at least foreign firms can hire and recruit staff directly, without their paying directly to the government.

Not so in Cuba, which is more like North Korea than it is Vietnam or China. A Cuban worker at the foreign-owned resort receives only a fraction of their salary, as little as 5 percent. So in the regimes that the Castro brothers or the Kim family run, the method is the same; extract hard currency for foreign businesses and invest it in the security apparatus.

Instead of dismantling a 50-year-old failed policy, as it claims, the administration may have given a 50-year-old failed regime a new lease on life to continue its repression at home and militant support for Marxist regimes abroad.

Before going to Mr. Engel, I am now going to yield my remaining time to Ileana Ros-Lehtinen, the chairman emeritus of this committee. Born in Havana, Chairman Ros-Lehtinen fled Cuba as a refugee at age 8. Her years of work on this committee have been marked by a tireless commitment to freedom and democracy for people around the world.

Ms. ROS-LEHTINEN. Thank you so much, Mr. Chairman, and I strongly second your grave concerns about the way that foreign policy is being run from the White House by secretly negotiating with the Castro regime while keeping the Congress, the American people, even our own diplomats in the dark.

This foreign policy decision is in line with the President's other examples of Executive overreach and bypassing consultations with Congress. Just like the Taliban 5 trade with Bergdahl, the President has established a dangerous precedent that the United States does, in fact, negotiate with terrorists, putting a target on every American's back and jeopardizing our national security.

Ever since the secret negotiations began of June 2013, this is what the Castro regime has been doing since day one of the talks as the U.S. establishes diplomatic relations. Just a few examples.

July 15, 2013, a North Korean flagged cargo ship called Chong Chon Gang was caught in Panama after it left Cuba heading to North Korea. After inspections, the shipment included various components of surface-to-air missile systems and launchers, MiG–21 jet fighter parts and engines, shell casings, rocket propelled projectiles as the cargo hide under 200,000 bags of sugar. October 6, 2013, over 135 democracy activists arrested in 1 day throughout Cuba. Also arrested was the leader of the Ladies in White, Berta Soler, who was dragged through the streets by her hair, and her husband, Angel Moya, was arrested.

November 4, 2013, a Cuban artist, a young man called Critico, was on the verge of death due to a hunger strike. January 24, 2014, Dr. Oscar Elias Biscet, arrested. He was awarded the Presidential Medal of Freedom by President Bush. June 12, 2014, Jorge Luis Garcia Perez Antunez and Yris Perez Aguilera, Ladies in White, leader Berta Soler and Angel Moya, and others arrested. July 16, 2014, Cuba and Russia agreed to reopen the Lourdes missile—the Lourdes spying facility. In fact, in 2014, Mr. Chairman, it led to almost 9,000 arrests of pro-democracy leaders in 1 year. Almost a 40-percent increase from 2013, while we were in negotiations.

In 2013, 2014 and last month, while the U.S. delegation arrived in Havana, Russia's spy ship docked in Cuba, and just last week, last week, the Castro regime sentenced a Cuban rapper, a young man known as El Dkano, to a 1-year prison sentence, and check out the charge: ``Dangerousness likely leading to a crime.'' That is an actual charge in Castro's Cuba. And 2 days ago, just to wrap it up, Mr. Chairman, a Cuban pro-democracy activist, Arelis Palacio, was brutally beaten all over her face and body, and she told state security, ``I would rather die than remain quiet and accept this.''

All of this happened while the U.S. was secretly negotiating with the Castro regime. Shame on us.

Thank you.

Chairman ROYCE. We go now to our ranking member, Mr. Eliot Engel of New York.

Mr. ENGEL. Thank you very much, Chairman Royce. Let me thank you, firstly, for calling this hearing. As a former chairman of the Western Hemisphere Subcommittee, I follow Cuba closely. For many years, I have worked with Ileana Ros-Lehtinen and others trying to bring freedom to Cuba.

Let me also thank our witnesses for their testimony today and for their dedicated service to our country. Thank you, to the three of you, for coming.

First and foremost I am delighted that Alan Gross is finally home after 5 long years. I first met his wife Judy back in December 2009. One of my sons went to school with one of the Gross' children. So I have always felt a connection to the Gross family. Alan's release from prison was long overdue, and I am overjoyed that he has been reunited with his family.

As we all know, President Obama announced several major changes in U.S. policy toward Cuba, but this is not the end of the story. The onus is now on the Cuban Government to respond by moving forward with real reform. And what exactly does this mean? To me it means free and fair elections, respect for the rule of law, an independent press, and upholding the values enshrined in the Inter-American Democratic Charter. It also means releasing each and every political prisoner currently jailed in Cuba and ending the harassment of political activists. We want to see the formation of political pluralism there. Only then will we be comfortable with Cuba moving along the path to democracy.

President Obama has the authority the reestablish relations with Cuba, and to make the regulatory changes that he announced on December 17. At the same time, however, Congress has the authority to maintain or eliminate the trade embargo on Cuba, and again, normalizing relations with Cuba cannot be a one-way street. It cannot be. It has got to be give and take on both sides, and at this time, I believe that Congress must see a greater political opening in Cuba before lifting the embargo.

Last month Chairman Royce and I sent a letter to Secretary Kerry. We asked for the names of the 53 political prisoners the Cuban Government committed to releasing. I was very grateful for Secretary Kerry's rapid response to our letter with a full list of the released prisoners. To be sure, the release of these 53 prisoners was a very positive step. Unfortunately, a few of these prisoners were subsequently detained because of their political activism. While these individuals are no longer in jail, we must be vigilant in ensuring their safety. I urge the State Department to use its talks with Cuban officials to continue pushing for the release of all political prisoners.

Finally, let me say that the upcoming Summit of the Americas in Panama presents an important opportunity for all of the countries in the region. We will be eager to hear from Cuban civil society leaders, along with other independent civil society leaders from throughout the Americas. I hope to be there, and I hope that we will have a delegation, a bipartisan delegation, going there too. I urge the Panamanian Government and all regional leaders to be as open and transparent as possible in allowing for civil society participation at the summit.

And one request before I close, Mr. Chairman, I ask unanimous consent to submit for the record two statements; one on behalf of Alan Gross, and the second from our colleague Representative Barbara Lee, a former Foreign Affairs committee member, along with her questions for the record.

Chairman ROYCE. Without objection.

Mr. ENGEL. Thank you, Mr. Chairman.

I would like to close again by thanking our witness for being here today. I look forward to hearing from each of you, and thank you again, Mr. Chairman, for holding this important hearing.

Chairman ROYCE. Thank you, Mr. Engel.

We go now to Mr. Jeff Duncan, chairman of the Subcommittee on Western Hemisphere for 1 minute.

Mr. DUNCAN. Thank you, Mr. Chairman, and in addition to the other comments, I remain deeply skeptical of the Obama administration's unilateral Cuba policy shift. In addition to circumventing Congress, failing to consult any Cuban dissidents or civil society, and ignoring the wisdom and advise of seasoned American foreign service officers, the President's made his decision to embark on a new course in Cuba, using political speech writers on the National Security Council staff to craft his policy change.

Mr. Chairman, I want to associate myself with your remarks and those of the gentlelady from Florida, Ms. Ros-Lehtinen, emphasizing my deep concern for the President's lack of transparency and the manner and process used to develop this policy change.

Yesterday, witnesses in testimony in the Senate hearing recognized that the Western Hemisphere—excuse me—recognized that Russia is one of the most—openly challenged the United States in regard to Cuba; these are external actors that have influence in the region.

And in view of the events that I thought the gentlelady from Florida spelled out, the U.S. must protect the United States' national security interest in any future negotiations with the Cuba Government, including maintaining U.S. permanent rights to the U.S. Naval station in Guantanamo Bay.

And with that, I yield back.

Chairman ROYCE. Thank you. I now recognize the ranking member of the Subcommittee on the Western Hemisphere who also is the one other Cuban-born member of this committee. Mr. Sires also was born in Havana. Were you about 11 when you——

Mr. SIRES. Yes.

Chairman ROYCE. Well, thank you. Mr. Albio Sires.

Mr. SIRES. Thank you, Mr. Chairman.

Yeah, I did come to this country when I was 11 years old in 1962, and I experienced some of this government's tactics, but I am—my biggest disappointment with this whole process has been that I always felt that the embargo and the pressure that we were putting on Cuba would lead to some changes in Cuba. I really don't see how what we negotiated is going to lead into anything. You know, it is just beyond me that a signature on a piece of paper somehow relieves this dictator of this pressure.

People are not going to benefit. You still have to go through the government for anything. Even if you want to put a church in Cuba, you have to go through the government. They have to okay this church. And do we think that we are going to be able to invest and do economic progress for the Cuban people? I don't see that happening.

And I would like to associate myself with the chairman's comments and my ranking member's.

I just don't see where we are headed with this. I know it is the last 2 years of the President. I know that he has a history to build, but I was disappointed in the fact that we are not using this as a pressure point on a government that has been so brutal. There are thousands of people in jail. I deal with these people today. My district has the second largest concentration of Cuban Americans in this country. I probably get more intel from the people on Hudson Avenue in Union City than I get from some of the briefings that I get in this place.

So I thank you, Mr. Chairman.

Chairman ROYCE. Thank you, Mr. Sires.

This morning we are pleased to be joined by witnesses from the Departments of State and Treasury and Commerce.

Ms. Roberta Jacobson is the Assistant Secretary of State for the Bureau of Western Hemisphere Affairs, and formerly served as the deputy assistant secretary for Canada and for Mexico.

Mr. John Smith is the Deputy Director of the U.S. Department of the Treasury's Office of Foreign Asset Control, that is OFAC, and previously he served as an expert to the United Nations Al-Qaida and Taliban Sanctions Committee from 2004 to 2007.

Mr. Matthew Borman currently serves as the Deputy Assistant Secretary of Commerce for Export Administration.

Without objection, the briefers' full prepared statements will be made part of the record. Members will have 5 calendar days to submit statements and questions and any extraneous material that any of these members of this committee want to put in the record.

So, Ms. Jacobson, if you would please summarize your remarks in 5 minutes, and than we will hear from the other two witnesses.

STATEMENT OF THE HONORABLE ROBERTA S. JACOBSON, AS-SISTANT SECRETARY, BUREAU OF WESTERN HEMISPHERE AFFAIRS, U.S. DEPARTMENT OF STATE

Ms. JACOBSON. Thank you very much, Chairman Royce, Ranking Member Mr. Engel, and members of the committee. And thank you for the opportunity to testify today on the new approach to U.S.-Cuba policy. I want to say that I appreciate this committee's engagement in the western hemisphere, and I know all of your strong commitments to democratic values, human rights, and social and economic opportunities in the Americas and in Cuba.

I want to thank you also for support in welcoming the long overdue return of Alan Gross to his family. During Mr. Gross' 5 long years of detention, the administration has worked closely with many Members of Congress in both Houses and from both parties to secure his release. As the President and the Secretary have said, we are also grateful for the essential roles of Canada, Pope Francis, and the Vatican in reaching an agreement that made Mr. Gross' freedom possible.

On December 17th, the President announced a new policy toward Cuba, one that will better enable us to effectively advance our values and help the Cuban people move into the 21st century. Other previous approaches to relations with Cuba over half a century, though rooted in the best of intentions, failed to empower the Cuban people. Instead, it isolated us from our democratic partners in this hemisphere and around the world. In addition, the Cuban Government used this policy as an excuse for restrictions on its citizens, and as a result, those most deprived were the Cuban people itself.

Our new approach is designed to promote every Cuban's universal rights, as well as our national interests, and we are already seeing signs that our updated approach gives us a greater ability to engage other nations in the hemisphere in advancing respect for fundamental freedoms in Cuba.

Ultimately, it will be the Cuban people who drive economic and political reforms. That is why we lifted restrictions to make it easier for Cuban Americans to travel and send remittances to their families in Cuba and open new pathways for academic, religious, and people-to-people exchanges. Our new steps build on this foundation by increasing authorized travel and commerce and the flow of information to, from, and within Cuba.

Nobody represents America's values better than the American people, and increased people-to-people contact will empower the Cuban people and reduce their dependency on the Cuban state.

The regulatory changes we announced will increase financial resources to support the Cuban people and the emerging Cuban private sector, and they enable U.S. companies to expand tele-communications and Internet access within Cuba. U.S. policy will no longer be a barrier to connectivity in Cuba.

Two weeks ago I made a historic trip to Cuba, one that helped me understand the burden and hope embodied in this policy when average Cubans and Cuban Americans wished me luck or said, ''God bless you,'' and encouraged our efforts. During talks, we were clear that our Governments have both shared interests and sharp differences. On practical issues, such as establishing direct mail service, counternarcotics, or oil spill mitigation, we agreed to continue dialogue and deepen cooperation, but this administration is under no illusions about the nature of the Cuban Government.

I also raised with Cuban officials our concerns about their harassment, use of violence, and arbitrary detention of Cuban citizens peacefully expressing their views. I met with dissidents, entrepreneurs, and independent media voices to talk about what they need from their government and from us.

We will continue to use our diplomatic efforts to encourage our allies, now more likely to work with us, to take every opportunity to support increased respect for human rights and fundamental freedoms in Cuba. As the President has said, the United States believes that no Cuban should face harassment, or arrest, or beatings simply because they are exercising a universal right to have their voices heard, and we will continue to support civil society there.

I encourage Members visiting Cuba to expand their engagement with independent civil society voices in Cuba. They offer us valuable insights and a diversity of views. And I raised several elements in Havana that presently inhibit the work of our U.S. intersection, including travel restrictions on our diplomats, limits on staffing, local access to the mission, and problems receiving shipments. The successful resolution of these issues will enable a future U.S. Embassy to provide services commensurate with our diplomatic missions around the world. I hope you won't object to having seen our diplomats in action most recently, if I take this opportunity to salute their tireless efforts to advance our interests on the island. They are dedicated public servants.

We have only just begun this effort to normalize relations, and we appreciate that there is a diversity of views in the U.S. Congress on this effort toward Cuba. We hope that we can work together to find common ground toward our shared goal of enabling the Cuban people to freely determine their own future.

Thank you very much.

Chairman ROYCE. Thank you.

[The prepared statement of Ms. Jacobson follows:]

"CUBA: ASSESSING THE ADMINISTRATION'S SUDDEN SHIFT"

TESTIMONY OF
ROBERTA S. JACOBSON
ASSISTANT SECRETARY OF STATE
BUREAU OF WESTERN HEMISPHERE AFFAIRS
U.S. DEPARTMENT OF STATE
BEFORE
THE HOUSE FOREIGN AFFAIRS COMMITTEE
UNITED STATES HOUSE OF REPRESENTATIVES
FEBRUARY 4, 2015

Chairman Royce, Ranking Member Engel, and Members of the Committee:

Thank you for the opportunity to testify today on our new approach to U.S.-Cuba policy. I know many of you have a deep interest in U.S. policy towards Cuba and have closely followed the President's announcement on December 17 and subsequent events, including my meetings in Havana two weeks ago. I appreciate the Committee's engagement on issues related to Cuba and the Western Hemisphere and applaud your strong commitment to democratic values, human rights, and expanding social and economic opportunity in the Americas.

I also want to thank the Committee for its assistance in welcoming the long-overdue return of Alan Gross to his family. During Mr. Gross' five long years of detention, the Administration worked closely with many members of Congress – from both chambers and from both parties – to secure his release. As the President and the Secretary have said, we are also grateful for the essential roles of Canada, Pope Francis, and the Vatican in reaching an agreement that made Mr. Gross' freedom possible.

Our previous approach to relations with Cuba over a half century, though rooted in the best of intentions, failed to empower the Cuban people and isolated us from our democratic partners in this hemisphere and around the world. Additionally, the Cuban government has used this policy as a rationale for restrictions on its people. As a result, unfortunately and unintentionally, those most deprived were the Cuban people.

The President's initiatives look forward and are designed to promote changes that support universal human rights and fundamental freedoms for every

Cuban, as well as changes that promote our other national interests. They emphasize the value of people-to-people contact and very specific forms of increased commerce. We are already seeing indications that our updated approach gives us a greater ability to engage other nations in the hemisphere and around the world in promoting respect for fundamental freedoms in Cuba. It has also drawn considerably greater attention to the actions and policies of the Cuban government.

From the beginning of this Administration, our approach has been to implement policies toward Cuba that support the Cuban people in freely determining their own future – their own political and economic future. Because ultimately, it will be the Cuban people themselves who drive political and economic reforms. That is why we lifted restrictions to make it easier for Cuban Americans to travel and send remittances to their families in Cuba, and opened new pathways for academic, religious, and people-to-people exchanges. These changes created powerful new connections between our two countries. The steps we are implementing now build on this foundation by increasing travel, authorized commerce, and the flow of information to, from, and within Cuba. The regulatory changes we announced will increase the financial resources to support the Cuban people and the emerging Cuban private sector. They also enable U.S. companies to expand telecommunications and internet access within Cuba. U.S. policy will no longer be a barrier to connectivity in Cuba.

This Administration is under no illusions about the continued barriers to internationally recognized freedoms that remain for the Cuban people, nor are we under illusions about the nature of the Cuban government. When we sat down with our counterparts in Havana, we were clear that our governments have both shared interests and sharp differences. From mail service to counter narcotics to oil spill mitigation, we owe our people a diplomatic relationship that allows an effective pursuit of their interests. On these types of practical issues, we agreed to continue dialogue and increase cooperation. At the same time, I raised with the Cuban government our concerns about its harassment, use of violence, and arbitrary detention of Cuban citizens peacefully expressing their views. I met with dissidents, entrepreneurs, and independent media voices to talk about what they need from their government and from us.

I talked with my Cuban counterpart about several elements that presently inhibit the work of our U.S. Interests Section, including travel restrictions on our diplomats, limits on staffing and local access to the mission, and problems receiving timely shipments to the mission. The successful resolution of these issues will enable a future U.S. Embassy to provide services commensurate with our other diplomatic missions around the world and on a par with the many foreign diplomatic missions in Cuba. We began a useful discussion and intend to meet again this month.

Having just seen our U.S. diplomats in Havana in action, I would like to take this opportunity to salute their tireless work to advance U.S. interests on the island by conducting educational and cultural diplomacy, monitoring significant political and economic developments, and promoting respect for democracy and human rights, including engaging with Cuba's independent civil society. These dedicated public servants have done their jobs under often very difficult circumstances. Our diplomats unite families through our immigration processing, provide American citizen services, and issue visas for qualified visitors to the United States. Our Refugee Processing Center provides assistance to victims of political repression. Our public diplomacy officers work in partnership with a range of journalists, including those from civil society, and provide hundreds of Cubans each week with uncensored internet access through our three Information Resource Centers. Our consular officers issue tens of thousands of travel documents annually to Cubans traveling to the United States for the purposes of emigrating or visiting friends and family. These efforts will continue and expand once we establish diplomatic relations with Cuba.

We have only begun the official talks on normalizing relations – which will take considerably longer than the first step, which is the re-establishment of diplomatic relations. But even while we do so, we will continue, both directly and through diplomatic channels, to encourage our allies to take every public and private opportunity to support increased respect for human rights and fundamental freedoms in Cuba. We will continue to use funds appropriated by Congress to support the exercise of political and civil liberties in Cuba, facilitate the free flow of information, and provide humanitarian assistance. We also look forward to increased engagement to empower the Cuban people through authorized contact with Members of Congress, U.S. government officials, and American travelers. We encourage Members visiting Cuba to expand their engagement with the independent voices in Cuban civil society and, whenever possible, to engage effectively on human rights and democracy with the Cuban government.

We will continue our discussions with our oversight and appropriations committees as we move toward a new relationship. We appreciate that there is a diversity of views in the U.S. Congress on the new direction towards Cuba. However, we hope that we can also work together to find common ground towards our shared goal of enabling the Cuban people to freely determine their own future.

We appreciate your attention to these important issues.

Thank you and I welcome your questions.

_____

Chairman ROYCE. Mr. Smith.

**STATEMENT OF MR. JOHN E. SMITH, DEPUTY DIRECTOR, OF-
FICE OF FOREIGN ASSETS CONTROL, U.S. DEPARTMENT OF
THE TREASURY**

Mr. SMITH. Thank you, Chairman Royce, Ranking Member
Engel, and members of the committee. Thank you for the invitation
to appear before you today to discuss our recent amendments to the
Cuban Assets Control Regulations. I will be addressing the key
changes we made to our regulations that Treasury's Office of Foreign Assets Control, or OFAC, made on January 16th to implement
the changes to U.S. policy toward Cuba announced by the President the month before. These amendments ease sanctions related
to Cuba in a number of key areas, including travel, remittances, financial services, and trade, and they are intended to have a direct
and positive impact on the lives of the Cuban people. Cuba is the
only OFAC sanctions program that restricts travel to a country.
The recent regulatory amendments ease the travel restrictions by
generally licensing certain travel within the 12 existing categories
of travel in our regulations. This means that the travelers who satisfy the criteria of the general licenses may travel to Cuba and conduct travel-related transactions there without requesting individual
authorization from OFAC. Travel to Cuba for tourist activities remains prohibited.

These expanded general licenses are intended to lessen the burden on authorized travelers, making it easier for Americans to
travel to Cuba to interact with the Cuban people, provide humanitarian assistance, and engage in certain educational and cultural
activities.

The regulatory amendments also authorize airlines to provide air
carrier services to, from, and within Cuba in connection with authorized travel. Air carriers wishing to provide services will still
need to secure regulatory approvals from other concerned U.S. Government agencies, such as the Departments of Transportation and
Homeland Security. Travel agents and tour group operators may
now also provide travel services in connection with authorized travel. These changes are intended to make authorized travel easier
and less expensive by reducing the paperwork burden for, and increasing competition among, those providing travel and carrier
services.

To improve the speed, efficiency, and oversight of authorized payments between the United States and Cuba, OFAC has authorized
U.S. banks to establish correspondent accounts at financial institutions in Cuba, and to allow travelers to use their credit and debit
cards while in Cuba.

Within the context of trade, OFAC has also modified the regulatory interpretation of the term "cash in advance," which describes
the financing requirement for trade between the United States and
Cuba that is imposed by statute. OFAC has now revised its interpretation of the term to allow the export of American-produced agricultural, medical, and other authorized goods to Cuba so long as
payment is received by the U.S. exporter prior to the goods' arrival
to a Cuban port. This change should increase authorized U.S. exports to Cuba.

Cuba has an Internet penetration of approximately 5 percent, one of the lowest in the world. In order to better facilitate the free flow of information to, from, and among the Cuban people, OFAC eased restrictions to better provide efficient and adequate telecommunications services between the United States and Cuba, and to increase access to telecommunications and Internet-based services for the Cuban people.

As I conclude, I should make one thing absolutely clear. Even with these changes I have described, most transactions between the United States and Cuba, most imports, most exports, and most other activities, remain prohibited. As OFAC implements these recent changes, we will continue to enforce the Cuba sanctions program vigorously, using all of our available tools, and take action against violators as appropriate.

The President's December 17th announcement laid out a new course for our relations with Cuba, driven by a hope for a more positive future for the Cuban people. OFAC's amendments to the regulations, in concert with the regulatory revisions my colleague at Commerce will highlight, mark significant changes to our Cuba sanctions policy that implement the new changes announced by the President. These changes are intended to directly benefit the Cuban people and help them to determine their own future.

Thank you, and I am happy to answer any questions.

[The prepared statement of Mr. Smith follows:]

Written Testimony on OFAC's Cuba Regulatory Changes of John E. Smith
Deputy Director of the Office of Foreign Assets Control
United States Department of the Treasury

United States House Foreign Affairs Committee

February 4, 2015

Good morning, Chairman Royce, Ranking Member Engel, and distinguished members of the committee. Thank you for the invitation to appear before you today to discuss our recent amendments to the Cuban Assets Control Regulations. I will be addressing the key regulatory amendments made by Treasury's Office of Foreign Assets Control (OFAC) to implement the changes to U.S. policy toward Cuba announced by the President, as well as the restrictions that remain in place. These regulatory changes ease Cuba sanctions within the continuing constraints of the embargo while advancing the Administration's policy to further engage and empower the Cuban people in their efforts to build a democratic, prosperous and stable Cuba.

On December 17, the President announced a number of significant policy changes regarding our relationship with Cuba. To implement these policy changes, OFAC amended the Cuban Assets Control Regulations on January 16. These amendments ease sanctions related to Cuba in a number of key areas, including travel, remittances, financial services, and trade. These changes are intended to have a direct and positive impact on the lives of the Cuban people. They are also aimed at enhancing both commerce and communications between the United States and Cuba, and helping the Cuban people to freely determine their own future.

Easing Travel Restrictions

Cuba is the only OFAC sanctions program that restricts travel to a country. The recent changes to the Cuba travel rules build on modifications previously made in 2009 and 2011. Those earlier changes, which were announced by the Administration and implemented by OFAC, eased travel restrictions with respect to Americans' ability to visit family and engage in educational, cultural, journalistic, and religious activities in Cuba.

The recent regulatory amendments ease travel restrictions further by generally licensing certain travel within the 12 existing categories of travel in OFAC's regulations, without the need for a specific license from OFAC. This means that travelers who satisfy the criteria of the general licenses set forth in OFAC's regulations may travel to Cuba and conduct travel-related transactions there without requesting individual authorization from OFAC. The 12 categories of travel are those referenced by Congress in the Trade Sanctions Reform and Export Enhancement Act (TSRA) of 2000. Travel to Cuba for tourist activities, which the TSRA statute defines as any activity outside of these 12 categories, remains prohibited.

These 12 categories of authorized travel are:

1. family visits;
2. official business of the U.S. government, foreign governments, and certain intergovernmental organizations;
3. journalistic activity;
4. professional research and professional meetings;
5. educational activities;
6. religious activities;
7. public performances, clinics, workshops, athletic and other competitions, and exhibitions;
8. support for the Cuban people;
9. humanitarian projects;
10. activities of private foundations or research or educational institutes;
11. exportation, importation, or transmission of information or information materials; and
12. certain authorized export transactions.

While certain previous general licenses authorized some travel within the 12 categories of travel, the additional and expanded general licenses that recently took effect are intended to lessen the burden on authorized travelers, making it easier for Americans to interact with the Cuban people, provide humanitarian assistance, engage in certain educational and cultural activities, and provide business training and resources for private Cuban businesses.

The recent regulatory amendments also authorize airlines to provide air carrier services to, from, and within Cuba, in connection with authorized travel. Air carriers wishing to provide service still will need to secure regulatory approvals from other concerned U.S. Government agencies, including the Departments of Transportation and Homeland Security. Persons subject to U.S. jurisdiction such as travel agents and tour group operators also may now provide travel services in connection with authorized travel. These changes are intended to make authorized travel easier and less expensive by reducing the paperwork burden for, and increasing competition among, those providing travel and air carrier services.

Change That Will Benefit the Cuban People: Remittances

Among the goals of the policy changes announced by the President is that of strengthening Cuban civil society. To facilitate this, OFAC eased certain restrictions on remittances to Cuba, following similar actions we took in 2009 and 2011. In 2009, OFAC authorized Americans to send unlimited amounts of remittances to their close relatives in Cuba, except for certain Cuban government and Communist Party officials. In 2011, OFAC authorized unlimited amounts of remittances for religious organizations in Cuba in support of religious activities. At that same time, OFAC also eased restrictions on certain other remittances to allow individuals in the United States to send up to $500 per quarter to any Cuban national, except for certain Cuban government and Communist Party officials.

In the recent amendments, OFAC increased that quarterly remittance limitation from $500 to $2,000 per person per quarter. OFAC also generally authorized remittances to certain individuals and independent non-governmental organizations in Cuba for humanitarian projects, support for the Cuban people, and the development of private businesses in Cuba, with no limitation on the amount. These changes are intended to facilitate the flow of authorized funds directly to the Cuban people to help promote self-employment and increased private property ownership, which in turn, strengthens an independent civil society.

Increasing Access to Financial Services

The President's policy announcement also focused on the need to advance political and economic freedom in Cuba through enhanced commerce and trade between the United States and Cuba, and empowering the nascent private sector. To improve the speed, efficiency, and oversight of authorized payments between the United States and Cuba, OFAC has authorized U.S. banks to establish correspondent accounts at financial institutions in Cuba and to allow travelers to use their credit and debit cards in Cuba. These changes will support those individuals and businesses engaged in authorized travel and trade with Cuba – for example, in the areas of agriculture, medicine and medical products, and communications – by facilitating authorized financial transactions.

Within the context of trade, OFAC also modified the regulatory interpretation of the term "cash-in-advance," which describes a financing requirement for trade between the United States and Cuba that is imposed by statute. This term dictates when authorized U.S. exporters to Cuba must receive payment for their goods. Previously, OFAC had interpreted that statutory term to mean that the U.S. exporter had to receive payment from the Cuban importer prior to the goods leaving U.S. shores – an interpretation that American exporters have said made their products less competitive than those from other countries. OFAC has now revised its interpretation of the term to mean that payment is required prior to transfer of title and control of goods. This permits the export of American-produced agricultural, medical, and other authorized goods to Cuba so long as payment is received by the U.S. exporter prior to the goods' arrival to a Cuban port. This change should increase authorized U.S. exports to Cuba, which in 2013 totaled more than $358 million in agricultural products, medical devices, medicine, and humanitarian items.

Telecommunications and the Free Flow of Information

Cuba has an Internet penetration of approximately five percent – one of the lowest in the world. Coupled with the exorbitant costs of telecommunications equipment, this has severely limited the ability of Cubans to communicate with each other and the outside world. In order to better facilitate the free flow of information to, from, and among the Cuban people, in accordance with the President's announcement, OFAC eased restrictions to better provide efficient and adequate telecommunications services between the United States and Cuba and to increase access to telecommunications and Internet-based services for the Cuban people. These steps build upon efforts initiated in 2009 to facilitate the free flow of information, and include the authorization for certain telecommunications and Internet-based services, and for facilities to provide telecommunications services linking the United States or third countries and Cuba, including facilities to provide telecommunications services within Cuba.

In coordination with our colleagues at the Commerce Department, OFAC also has authorized certain services incident to Internet-based communications and those related to exportations and reexportations of certain communications items. This means, for example, that transactions related to fee-based Internet communications services, such as e-mail, social networking, web-hosting, or domain-name registration are now authorized in most circumstances. Services related to many kinds of software (including applications) used on personal computers, cell phones, and other personal communications devices are also authorized. Additionally, services related to certain authorized exports, such as cloud storage, software design, business consulting, and the provision of information technology management and support related to the use of hardware and software exported or reexported to Cuba pursuant to Commerce Department rules are permitted. These changes will facilitate increased communication to, from, and within Cuba and will facilitate multiple avenues for the free flow of information and ideas to ordinary Cubans.

Supporting Diplomacy

The President also announced his decision to begin discussions with Cuba to reestablish diplomatic relations. To facilitate that process, OFAC authorized transactions with Cuban official missions and their employees in the United States. In addition, in an effort to support U.S. government interests, OFAC authorized Cuba-related transactions by employees, grantees, and contractors of the U.S. government and certain intergovernmental organizations in their official capacities.

Conclusion

As I conclude, I should make one point absolutely clear: Even with these changes I've described, most transactions between the United States and Cuba – including most export, import, and other activities – remain prohibited. OFAC will continue to enforce these prohibitions, using all of our available tools. Persons traveling to or engaging in transactions involving Cuba will continue to be required to maintain records for five years, thereby allowing OFAC to access information relevant to possible enforcement actions. In fiscal year 2014, for example, civil penalties and monetary settlements related to OFAC enforcement actions involving Cuba totaled over $35 million. As OFAC implements these recent changes, we will continue to enforce the Cuba sanctions program vigorously and take actions against violators, as appropriate.

The President's December 17 announcement laid out a new course for our relations with Cuba, driven by a hope for a more positive future for the Cuban people. OFAC's regulatory amendments to the Cuban Assets Control Regulations, in concert with the regulatory revisions my colleague at Commerce will highlight, mark significant changes to our Cuba sanctions that implement the new policy announced by the President. These changes are intended to directly benefit the Cuban people and help them to freely determine their own future.

Thank you. I welcome your questions.

STATEMENT OF MR. MATTHEW S. BORMAN, DEPUTY ASSISTANT SECRETARY OF COMMERCE FOR EXPORT ADMINISTRATION, BUREAU OF INDUSTRY AND SECURITY, U.S. DEPARTMENT OF COMMERCE

Mr. BORMAN. Mr. Chairman, Ranking Member Engel, members of the committee, thank you for the opportunity to appear before the committee today to describe the Department of Commerce's regulatory revisions to implement the Cuba policy changes announced by the President on December 17th.

As the President noted, these changes are intended to create more opportunities for the American and Cuban people, promote positive change in Cuba, and influence outcomes throughout the western hemisphere.

On January 16th, the Department of Commerce's Bureau of Industry and Security (BIS) amended the Export Administration Regulations to authorize the export and re-export of certain items to Cuba that are intended to improve the living conditions of the Cuban people, support private sector economic activity, strengthen civil society in Cuba, and improve the free flow of information to, from, and among the Cuban people.

BIS amended the regulations to expand two existing general authorizations, or license exceptions in the Commerce regulations, create a new license exception, and describe a licensing policy.

Under the embargo on trade with Cuba, all items that are subject to Commerce regulations require a license for export or re-export to Cuba unless authorized by a license exception. BIS administers export and re-export restrictions on Cuba consistent with the goals of the embargo and with relevant laws. Thus, BIS may issue licenses for specific transactions or make types of transactions eligible for license exceptions that support the goals of the United States' policy while the embargo is in effect. Only items of lower technological sensitivity that are subject to limited export restrictions are eligible for these license exceptions.

The first license exception that was expanded is the license exception related to gift parcels. The change here is to allow consolidated shipments of gift parcels to go under this license exception. Previously they required individual licenses. This change will enable more donations to the Cuban people because individuals who wish to donate eligible items to the Cuban people will no longer have to search for a license consolidator.

BIS also expanded license exception Consumer Communications Devices (CCD) to now also authorize the commercial sale of commercial communication devices such as cell phones, mobile phones, computers, radios, and digital cameras. Previously these were only authorized under the license exception if they were donated. Now they can also be sold commercially.

The new license exception that we created is Support for the Cuban People, or SCP. This license exception enables the export and re-export to Cuba of items intended to empower the nascent Cuban private sector by supporting private economic activity. Authorized items include building materials for private sector use, tools and equipment for private sector agricultural activity, and goods for use by private sector entrepreneurs such as auto mechanics, barbers, hair stylists, and restaurateurs. This license exception is intended to meet the President's goal of supporting the Cuban private sector and facilitate Cuban citizens' lower-priced access to certain goods to improve their living standards and gain greater economic independence from the state.

Other provisions of the license exception SCP authorize the temporary export by persons leaving the United States of items for their use in archeological, cultural, ecological, educational, historic preservation, scientific, or sporting activities. It authorizes the export and re-export of certain donated items for use by the Cuban people engaged in the activities I just mentioned, and the export and re-export of items to human rights organizations, individuals, or nongovernment organizations that promote independent civil activity.

These provisions implement the President's goals of harnessing the power of people-to-people engagement and of helping the Cuban people reach for a better future.

As the President observed, nobody represents America's values better than the American people.

To implement the President's goal of empowering the Cuban people by increasing their access to information, particularly through the Internet, and their ability to communicate with one another and with people in the United States and the rest of the world, license exception SCP authorizes the export to Cuba of items for the establishment and upgrade of telecommunications-related systems, in addition to the consumer communication devices authorized by license exception CCD. A related provision of license exception SCP authorizes the export and re-export to Cuba of certain items for use by news media personnel and U.S. news bureaus engaged in the gathering and dissemination of news to the general public.

Lastly, this rule recognizes that environmental threats are not limited by national borders, and circumstances may warrant the export or re-export of certain items to Cuba to protect the U.S. and international air quality, water quality, and coastlines. Although pre-existing licensing policy provided the flexibility necessary to authorize such transactions, we have now amended the regulations to make explicit the general policy of approving such exports.

In summary, these regulatory revisions implement the President's recently announced Cuba policy changes consistent with the comprehensive embargo the United States maintains on trade with Cuba. The changes support the President's goal of the United States becoming a better partner in making the lives of ordinary Cubans a little bit easier and more free, and is in line with U.S. national security interests. And I would also be pleased to answer questions.

Thank you.

Chairman ROYCE. Thank you. Thank you.

[The prepared statement of Mr. Borman follows:]

Statement of

Matthew S. Borman
Deputy Assistant Secretary of Commerce for Export Administration

before the

Committee on Foreign Affairs
United States House of Representatives

February 4, 2015

Mr. Chairman, Ranking Member Engel, Members of the Committee:

Thank you for the opportunity to appear before the Committee today to describe the
Department of Commerce's regulatory revisions to implement the Cuba policy changes
announced by the President on December 17, 2014. As the President noted, these changes are
intended to create more opportunities for the American and Cuban people, promote positive
change in Cuba, and influence outcomes throughout the Western Hemisphere. On January 16,
2015, the Department of Commerce's Bureau of Industry and Security (BIS) amended the Export
Administration Regulations (EAR) to authorize the export and reexport of certain items to Cuba
that are intended to improve the living conditions of the Cuban people; support private sector
economic activity and strengthen civil society in Cuba; and improve the free flow of information
to, from, and among the Cuban people.

BIS amended the EAR to expand two existing general authorizations (license exceptions
in the EAR), create a new license exception, and describe a licensing policy. Under the
embargo on trade with Cuba, all items subject to the EAR require a license for export or reexport
to Cuba unless authorized by a license exception. BIS administers export and reexport
restrictions on Cuba consistent with the goals of that embargo and with relevant law.
Thus, BIS may issue licenses for specific transactions or make types of transactions eligible for

license exceptions that support the goals of United States policy while the embargo is in effect. Only items of lower technological sensitivity that are subject to limited export restrictions are eligible for the license exceptions.

One of the license exceptions BIS amended is Gift Parcels and Humanitarian Donations (GFT). GFT generally authorizes the donation of gift parcels by an individual to an individual, or a religious, charitable or educational organization for the use of the recipient or the recipient's immediate family. License Exception GFT previously excluded consolidated shipments of gift parcels but now authorizes such shipments without a license. This change will enable more donations to the Cuban people by simplifying the process to export and reexport gift parcels to Cuba. Individuals who wish to donate eligible items to the Cuban people will no longer have to search for a licensed consolidator.

Another license exception BIS amended is Consumer Communications Devices (CCD). License Exception CCD previously only authorized the export or reexport of donated consumer communications devices, including personal computers, mobile phones, televisions, radios and digital cameras, and related software without a license. As amended, CCD now also authorizes commercial sales of consumer communications devices as well. BIS also updated License Exception CCD to track more precisely current technical specifications for consumer communications devices. Under CCD, the Cuban people will have greater access to consumer items widely available for retail purchase elsewhere in the world. This access will enhance their ability to obtain information, and to communicate with each other and the rest of the world, helping to bring Cuba into the 21st century.

The new license exception BIS created is Support for the Cuban People (SCP). This license exception enables the export and reexport to Cuba of items intended to empower the nascent Cuban private sector by supporting private economic activity. Authorized items include:

1) building materials for use by the private sector to construct or renovate privately-owned buildings including privately-owned residences, businesses, places of worship and buildings for private sector social or recreational use;

2) tools and equipment for private sector agricultural activity; and

3) goods for use by private sector entrepreneurs such as auto mechanics, barbers and hairstylists and restaurateurs;

This license exception is intended to meet the President's goal of supporting the Cuban private sector. These categories of items, intended to stimulate economic activity generated by private individuals and groups as enterprises for profit, may be commercially sold or donated. This license exception is intended to facilitate Cuban citizens' lower-priced access to certain goods to improve their living standards and gain greater economic independence from the state.

In addition, License Exception SCP contains provisions covering the export and reexport to Cuba of items for use in specified activities that can strengthen civil society in Cuba. SCP authorizes the *temporary* export by persons departing the United States of items for their use in archaeological, cultural, ecological, educational, historic preservation, scientific or sporting activities and the export and reexport of certain *donated* items for use by Cuban people engaged in those activities. SCP also authorizes the export and reexport of items to human rights organizations, individuals, or non-governmental organizations that promote independent activity intended to strengthen civil society in Cuba. These provisions implements the President's goals

25

of harnessing the "power of people-to-people engagement" and of helping the Cuban people "reach for a better future." As the President observed, "nobody represents America's values better than the American people."

To implement the President's goal of empowering the Cuban people by increasing their access to information (particularly through the Internet) and their ability to communicate with one another and with people in the United States and the rest of the world, License Exception SCP authorizes the export to Cuba of items for the establishment and upgrade of communications-related systems, in addition to the consumer communications devices, related software, applications, and hardware authorized by License Exception CCD. License Exception SCP also authorizes the export and reexport to Cuba of certain items for use by news media personnel and U.S. news bureaus engaged in the gathering and dissemination of news to the general public.

Lastly, this rule establishes a licensing policy related to environmental protection. This policy recognizes that environmental threats are not limited by national borders and circumstances may warrant the export or reexport of certain items to Cuba to protect U.S. and international air quality, waters, and coastlines. Although pre-existing licensing policy provided the flexibility necessary to authorize transactions related to environmental protection, BIS has amended the EAR to make explicit a general policy of approval for the export or reexport of these items.

In summary, BIS has amended the EAR to implement the President's recently announced Cuba policy changes consistent with the comprehensive embargo the United States maintains on trade with Cuba. The rule published in the *Federal Register* on January 16, 2015 makes a significant contribution toward achieving the President's goal of the United States becoming a better "partner in making the lives of ordinary Cubans a little bit easier . . . and more free" and is in line with U.S. national security interests.

I would be pleased to answer any questions you may have.

Chairman ROYCE. I would like to go to Assistant Secretary Jacobson with a question, because administration negotiators stated that they did not seek human rights concessions in exchange for taking steps toward normalization; and now you know our concern about the State Department and you not being included in this on the front end, being kept in the dark on it, but the reality is that pro-democracy and human rights activists in Cuba have lamented that human rights weren't integral to these secret negotiations. In fact, the lead Cuban Government negotiator, who would be now your counterpart, he said, ''Change in Cuba is not negotiable.'' We have no, you know, indication here that the Cuban Government intends to give ground, and so if the regime refuses to ease its repression on the people in Cuba, how do our concessions advance the interests of the Cuban people?

Ms. JACOBSON. Let me be clear, Mr. Chairman, on part of this. I think it is crucial to understand that there really were no concessions from the Obama administration. Moving forward with the establishment of diplomatic relations is not a gift or a concession to governments. It is a channel of communication. As you know, having Embassies in countries is often not seen by governments as a gift. Quite the contrary. We are quite irritating to governments sometimes, and in fact, it is not necessarily something that the Cuban Government wanted, but we think it is—the things that were announced on December 17th are a much more effective way to pursue our own national interests.

So we believe that we can more effectively pursue the human rights policies, and the democracy policies that we want in empowering the Cuban people, and in having that direct channel with the Cuban Government to convey those concerns and to work with allies around the hemisphere who no longer fear association with a policy they did not support because of this policy.

Chairman ROYCE. Well, but if I could just point out, what you are leaving out of the equation here is the fact that under these initiatives that the White House took without the State Department, but the White House took, the White House is now increasing the amount of dollars that flow into Cuba, specifically, these flow into the regime and helps the regime's bottom line at a time when the regime, as you could have told the White House, is now—now faces being cut off in terms of the subsidy from Venezuela. So at the very time that you think we would exert leverage, you have a situation instead where you have got sort of a lifeline. I mean, that is—that is my concern.

Let me go to another question I had, and that is last week, Raul Castro stated that normalizing bilateral relations with the U.S. would not be possible until the U.S. returns the Naval station at Guantanamo Bay to Cuba. Is the administration considering transferring this military asset back to the Cuban people? And I will remind you, when we talked with the State Department before on negotiations on another subject, the State Department spokesman said unequivocally that the United States is not considering the release of any member of the Cuban 5, one of whom was convicted for his part in killing four Americans, for Alan Gross. So we have got a little history of hearing one thing and then finding out another after the fact. But on this question on Guantanamo if you could——

Ms. JACOBSON. Sure. The issue of Guantanamo is not on the table in these conversations. I want to be clear that what we are talking about right now is the re-establishment of diplomatic relations, which is only one first step in normalization. Obviously the Cuban Government has raised Guantanamo. We are not interested in discussing that. We are not discussing that issue or a return of Guantanamo.

We also, I want to be clear, you know, we didn't return the Cuban agents for Mr. Gross. We returned the Cuban agents for an intelligence agent that we wanted back.

Chairman ROYCE. Let me ask you one last question. For years the Castro regime has perceived broadcasting by our Office of Cuba Broadcasting as a threat. Last week the Cuban Government referred to these as illegal, and Castro has demanded that the broadcast be stopped.

To what extent have our broadcasts been discussed as part of these talks?

Ms. JACOBSON. The Cuban Government has always raised radio and TV Marti both in the migration talks, and they raised them again as part of a list of things that they object to in the normalization talks, but we have no plans to end those either.

Chairman ROYCE. Well, I know that Cuba is demanding that they be shut down. I am hoping to hear you say that we are demanding that Cuba drop its jamming. But thank you. I am going to go to Mr. Engel because my time is up. Thank you.

Mr. ENGEL. Thank you.

Secretary Jacobson, let me just give you a broad leeway, because you have answered some of this, but I want to hear more. How do you answer the critics who say that we gave away the store? That we have—we had leverage and we just tossed it away. Didn't get concessions in exchange, and if we didn't, doesn't it show you the true intentions of the Castro regime? Raul Castro has reportedly said—touted the fact that he gave up nothing, and essentially we made all the concessions. How do you answer that?

Ms. JACOBSON. I appreciate the question, Congressman. I really do, because I think it is important—there is nothing in what we decided on the 17th that we believe is a concession to the Cuban Government. It is true that we have begun to talk about diplomatic relations. It is also true that we are going to try and move forward with Embassies in each other's countries. We strongly believe that having an Embassy in Havana will enable us to do more things that help us more effectively empower the Cuba people, not high necessarily on the Cuban Government's list of desires.

We also believe that by allowing American companies to engage in telecommunications sales and acting to get greater information into Cuba to work with the entrepreneurs who I sat down with while I was there, we can begin to increase the pace at which people separate themselves from the state, also not something that the Cuban Government has on its list of priorities. I think that they may tout this as support for their government, but we have diplomatic relations with lots of governments around the world with whom we sharply disagree. It is a channel. It is a mechanism. It is not, as somebody said yesterday on the Senate side, it is not the Good Housekeeping Seal of Approval, and we will continue to speak out on human rights, to support democracy activists, but we believe that this policy had become such an irritant in our work with other Latin American countries, with our European allies, that it also enables us to work more effectively with them in bringing about that support in Cuba.

Mr. ENGEL. Well, thank you. I mentioned in my statement that I was pleased with the release of the 53 political prisoners, but obviously much more remains to be done on the human rights front in Cuba. The Havana-based Cuban Commission on Human Rights and National Reconciliation reported 8,899 short term detentions in the year 2014, and that was a 39-percent increase over 2013.

So what is the Obama administration's strategy for pushing the Cuban Government to improve its human rights record? Are we working with other governments in the region and in the European Union to urge the Cuban Government to put an end to short-term detentions and harassment of dissidents?

Ms. JACOBSON. I think that is a really important point, because I think this question of short-term detentions is a crucial one. We obviously have seen a shift from longer-term sentences to short-term detentions. That number has gone way up in the last year. It is of enormous concern to us, and we have made it clear both to the Cuban Government directly now in these talks and others, and also with allies to international organizations that it is unacceptable. We do believe, and we have had those conversations already, that the new policy enables us to work better with other governments. The reaction of many governments in the region was: We strongly support your policy shift. It has changed the dynamic. What can we do to help? As we prepare for the Summit of the Americas, which you mentioned, we believe that Cuban civil society activists and independent human rights activists will have an opportunity to interact with Latin American leaders for the first time. All of those things, I think, will help.

That same national commission has noticed a drop in short-term detentions in January. Not a trend. I want to be clear about that. We cannot know whether that is the beginning of a trend, and we will be watching that very carefully because it must end. Not just come down, but it must end.

Mr. ENGEL. Well, you mentioned civil society. I want to ask my final question about civil society and the Summit of the Americas. What conversations have you had with your Panamanian counterparts to ensure that there is robust participation from Cuban civil society at the Summit of the Americas, and then in your discussions with Cuban Government officials in Havana, did you urge them to allow for civil society leaders from the island to participate in the summit? Did you encourage Cuban political dissidents to participate in the summit?

Ms. JACOBSON. The answer to all those questions is yes. We have had extensive conversations with the Panamanian Government, with the nongovernmental organizations that will be organizing the civil society forum, with other NGOs around the hemisphere, including in the United States, as well as making sure that the rules for the civil society summit are not the same as in previous years.

Previously it had been that you could only participate if you were an NGO registered with the OAS, which would preclude Cuban independent organizations. That will not be the case this year so that Cuban dissidents and independent organizations may be invited.

Mr. ENGEL. Thank you.

Thank you, Mr. Chairman.

Chairman ROYCE. We go now to Ileana Ros-Lehtinen.

Ms. ROS-LEHTINEN. Thank you so much, Mr. Chairman.

As we know, the U.S. has been negotiating in secret with this sadistic dictatorship for now 20 months, because it is still secret. For 18 of those months, the White House negotiated in super secret to trade three convicted spies for an innocent American. Even if you say that that was not a swap, that is just so disingenuous.

Assistant Secretary Jacobson, this week in the Senate, just yesterday, you testified, ''This policy is not based on the Castro regime changing,'' and you have said more or less that now, ''we have no illusions over that.''

So let me get this straight. We are telegraphing to the Castro regime ahead of time that it doesn't have to change. We have no illusions that it is going to change. So we are going to get further concessions from this administration. What is the point of negotiations, then, if we say we are negotiating, we have no illusions, let's see where this leads us?

Now, the media has been reporting just this week that arrests in Cuba for last month in January decreased to only 178, making it seem like the arrest of peaceful pro-democracy activists, 178 of them, is a low number. Only in Castro's Cuba could the arrest of 178 people in 1 month be considered a victory.

Now, for the President's State of the Union address last month, I invited Marlene Alejandre, the daughter of our Armando Alejandre. They were also kept in the dark about this trade/non-trade, this swap/non-swap. Her father was murdered by the Castro regime when his Brothers to the Rescue plane was shot down over international waters, and on December 17th, the President released and pardoned Gerardo Hernandez, a Cuban spy who was convicted in our U.S. courts for conspiracy to commit murder for his connection to the shootdown.

So the Alejandre family wanted me to ask you these questions, Assistant Secretary Jacobson: How will I explain to my three little girls that their U.S. Marine Vietnam veteran grandfather was denied the only justice for his murder when Gerardo Hernandez was set free, pardoned, and returned to Cuba? Next question: Why was the U.S. so willing to give Gerardo Hernandez the opportunity to father a child while he was in prison? Very interesting, when some of the victims of the shootdown will never be able to have children of their own.

Now as if negotiating in secret is not bad enough, the Castro regime continues to defy this administration, as the chairman has pointed out and the ranking member, setting preconditions publicly on the negotiations, such as demanding the return of the land of Guantanamo, which is so vital to U.S. national security interests. It is so pathetic for this strong, wonderful, generous country to look so weak when negotiating with the Castro regime.

Isn't it true that Cuba owes American taxpayers at least $8 billion in certified claims for the unlawful taking of property, of businesses, of unpaid debts owed to the American citizens? Isn't it true that Cuba has failed to pay these claims for close to 60 years, and isn't it true that U.S. law requires that these claims be resolved before relations be normalized?

So I urge all of your departments to explain how illegally confiscated properties will be resolved. U.S. claim holders deserve their claims to be protected. Don't you agree? And, Assistant Secretary Jacobson, it is important to note what the Castro regime will do with this new assistance that President Obama is going to provide on telecommunications.

Now, in 2012, Pope Benedict visited the island, as you know. The Castro regime responded with rounding up and arresting hundreds of civil society individuals, and he blocked the phones of the opposition leaders, and as we know, Castro held an American jailed for 5 years for trying to provide Internet equipment to the Jewish community in Cuba. So the track record is clear about Castro and his hatred of this telecommunication equipment, and in this latest misguided talks, the Castro regime asked the U.S. Interests Section to stop providing Internet services for the Cuban people. So his track record is clear. It has no intent of opening up the Internet or telecommunications opportunities. In fact, if given that opportunity, it is probably going to be used to further oppress the people of Cuba.

And then just one last thing, and you can answer it whenever you can in writing. Did Secretary Kerry lie to the United States Congress when he told us that we would not free up these convicted murder—these convicted spies, or was he kept out of the dark of these negotiations? And were you part of the negotiations from the start, or did you enter them later on? But I have run out of time.

Thank you.

Chairman ROYCE. Well, I am just going to suggest a little response in writing, and that way we can go to Mr. Brad Sherman of California.

Mr. SHERMAN. Thank you.

It is said that our policy toward Cuba for the last 50 years has failed. This comes from an American view that it is all about us, that the only thing—that if Cuba isn't better, it must be our policy that would have been the difference. Our policy is exactly different, or has been for the last 50 years, than Europe and Canada's policy. Maybe it is their policy that failed to bring democracy to Cuba, maybe it is ours.

Ms. Jacobson, Cuba got caught smuggling 240 tons of weapons to North Korea, violating U.N. sanctions. Cuba is not cooperating in the U.N. investigation. Are these reasons to keep Cuba on the State Sponsors of Terrorism List?

Ms. JACOBSON. Congressman, we are undertaking the review of the State Sponsors of Terrorism List right now. We are evaluating all of the information.

Mr. SHERMAN. I know that. Please.

Ms. JACOBSON. We also made clear when we were looking at that incident with the Chong Chon Gang that we did not think Cuba's— we did think Cuba's behavior violated the sanctions regime. The only entity that was sanctioned, as you know, as a result of that investigation was the North Korean company, which can no longer operate.

Mr. SHERMAN. I have got to reclaim my time. I have got——

Ms. JACOBSON. Okay.

Mr. SHERMAN [continuing]. So many questions.

Ms. Jacobson, Americans paid in blood for Cuban independence. We got a base in Guantanamo that is valuable to our national security. Are you prepared, and hopefully this is a yes-or-no question, to say right now: This administration will not abandon, return, or fail to pay the modest fee so that we can have that Naval base for the next 2 years?

Ms. JACOBSON. I don't see that discussion taking place.

Mr. SHERMAN. That is not what I am asking for. That was in your testimony.

What—can you make a commitment—because you have got to see it from our side here. We were shocked. So you telling me that you are not thinking of something means I got to get ready to get shocked tomorrow.

The administration was so angry that they hadn't been consulted on bringing one guy to speak here—it was not a lot of consultation on this huge change in Cuba policy.

Would the administration object to language in an appropriations bill designed to make it impossible for this administration to give back the Naval base?

Ms. JACOBSON. That issue is not on the table with the——

Mr. SHERMAN. Would the—it could be—it could be on our table. Would you object?

Ms. JACOBSON. I don't know the answer to that as it is a matter of Executive policy.

Mr. SHERMAN. Okay. Let me go on to Mr. Smith. We have got the Cuban Liberty and Democracy Solidarity Act. It doesn't allow us to deal with certain properties that have been seized by Americans. You have got new regulations on travel, credit cards, et cetera. How do you plan to make sure that American travelers aren't breaking the law by staying at hotels that were confiscated from Americans or otherwise violating the Cuban Liberty and Democracy Solidarity Act?

Mr. SMITH. One thing I should say at the start about that, the act, though, is that the act—what that does is say that you can't provide a loan or credit or provide financing to further those transactions involving confiscated property. It doesn't say that you can't have—you can't stay at a hotel or engage in any other kind of activities.

Mr. SHERMAN. Does the credit card company extend a loan when you use a credit card to pay for a hotel stay at a confiscated property?

Mr. SMITH. A credit card company may extend a loan to the traveler when you stay there.

Mr. SHERMAN. So you are extending the loan to facilitate staying at the hotel. You think that is in conformity with the act?

Mr. SMITH. Certainly. We have the provision of the act that is replicated in our regulations. We will follow to the letter what is in the act, because we have it in our regulations. We will follow that. But nothing that we have authorized would abridge those provisions of the act.

Mr. SHERMAN. I would just close by saying I might be more favorably impressed by the policy if it hadn't been such a complete shock and if Congress had been involved, and this U.S. Government will work better if we coordinate on foreign policy and have one national foreign policy that reflects the views of both elected bodies instead of a view of Congress as simply an annoying body that has to be consulted now, and then. I yield back.

Chairman ROYCE. We go now to Mr. Chris Smith of New Jersey.

Mr. SMITH OF NEW JERSEY. Thank you so much, Mr. Chairman, for calling this extraordinarily important hearing. You know, I say to our distinguished witnesses, and welcome to the committee, The Washington Post has done several editorials, one, Obama Gives the Castro Regime in Cuba an Undeserved Bailout, pointing out that with the Soviet Union and certainly now Venezuela less able to prop them up, now potentially U.S. funds will do that. Secondly, President Obama's Betrayal of Cuban Democrats, and the fact that we should have listened to Berta Soler, the Ladies in White, who will be testifying here tomorrow at a hearing I am chairing. She, along with Antunez and Ms. Fonseca, two of those are going back, two of those individuals. Talk about bravery, speaking to the Senate, now speaking to the House, and they are going back. And yet the Post, which is hardly a conservative bastion, talks about a betrayal of Cuban democrats. And in another editorial it said with no consequences in site, Cuba continues to crack down on free speech.

I would ask you, if you would, now an assessment, since it has been in effect, the negotiations and the publicity or visibility of them, are there any second thoughts? And I say that, 2012, Ileana Ros-Lehtinen and I had a hearing, and we heard from Dr. Biscet, who spent 11 years in prison. And the same type of scenario is playing out for even some of the 53 that were freed. Five have been rearrested. He was in and out of prison constantly. It is part of the harassment and the modus operandi, and we understand, and maybe you can verify it, that some 100 to 200 additional prisoners over the last 6 weeks have been arrested.

Is that true or is that is not? Some comments have been made that the ICRC may get to go to Cuba. That is not the issue. They need to go to the prisons, and the last time Armando Valladares was able to negotiate that, when he walked point in the 1990s, and I was with him in Geneva at the Human Rights Commission, when he secured that, representatives went into the prisons, interviewed people; and everybody, including family members, were severely retaliated against. The ICRC has to have unfettered access to the prisons. Meeting with Fidel Castro or anybody under him just doesn't cut it. I would like to go again. I have tried repeatedly. Madam Secretary, maybe you can help facilitate that. I want to go to the prisons and lead a delegation to the prisons. I have been to prisons in the Soviet Union. I have been to prisons in East bloc countries, as well as in Asia. Cuba is the one that won't let me or others into the prisons. Please help us with that. If you could answer those questions.

Let me ask you, in the negotiations there are many convicted felons, including Joanne Chesimard who gunned down Werner

Foerster in my State in cold blood, shot in the back of the head gangland style having escaped from prison, convicted, a fugitive felon, and yet she got asylum there. Was that part of the negotiations, the discussions, or was it not?

Finally, just let me ask with regards to, with the time I have, please answer those, and I will come back.

Ms. JACOBSON. Okay. Let me say that the whole point of this new policy is not that we are telescoping to the Cuban Government that they don't have to change or that we expect them to change right away. Certainly we want those practices to change. We simply are not naive about how quickly they may change, and so our efforts are to empower the Cuban people to take their lives into their own hands. I had not heard that 100 to 200 people had been arrested. There were certainly as many as 50 or more arrested around the time of Tania Bruguera, performance artist. To the best of my knowledge, most, if not all, have been released, although there are severe constraints on them; and none of them should have been arrested, just as there are still political prisoners in Cuba who should be released. I want to be clear about that, and the fact that a downturn in detentions is not good enough——

Mr. SMITH OF NEW JERSEY. The game they play, Madam Secretary, is that they arrest, rearrest and let out. Like when Antunez goes back. Seventeen years in prison. He has been tortured.

Ms. JACOBSON. Right. I completely agree.

Mr. SMITH OF NEW JERSEY. Dr. Biscet testified here by way of phone, and he said don't lift the embargo because you have got to get real substantive concessions.

Ms. JACOBSON. Agreed, and I saw Oscar Biscet when I was on the island, and I have the utmost respect and admiration for him and his views on this. Let me also say that every time I talk with the Cuban Government, I mention the case of Joanne Chesimard. I am a daughter of New Jersey. I grew up with this case and other fugitive cases.

Mr. SMITH OF NEW JERSEY. What is their response?

Ms. JACOBSON. We have not gotten a positive response on Joanne Chesimard.

Mr. SMITH OF NEW JERSEY. What did they say?

Ms. JACOBSON. They have said that they are not interested in discussing her return. Now, on other cases, we have made some more progress. There have been felons, accused felons, expelled to the United States. This is a very high priority for us, and we are frustrated that we have not made progress. There are other cases that we will continue; all of these cases, we will continue to pursue. We are going to have further dialogue on fugitives and law enforcement because this is critical to us. That is part of what we hope we will do better on in having conversations that are more expansive with our Justice Department colleagues. This is a critical part of having a channel.

Mr. SMITH OF NEW JERSEY. Just one last thing. We all know the Castro brothers have pushed this as a major diplomatic win for them. I would have hoped, and I think we all would have hoped, that human rights concessions would have been first before being recognized diplomatically.

Chairman ROYCE. We go now to Mr. Greg Meeks of New York.

Mr. MEEKS. Thank you, Mr. Chairman. Madam Secretary, it is good being with you. Let me first go on record as saying that I wholeheartedly agree with the President's change in direction. I think that it is clear that over 50 years, nothing has changed with the policy that we had, and time says that you don't do the same thing over and over again and you get the same result. So I wholeheartedly agree and think that the time is finally there for a change in policy. I should also say that I do feel the passion of, for example, my good friend, the ranking member of the Western Hemisphere in listening to his opening statement, because clearly the passion that he has is for the people of Cuba. And in listening to his opening statement, you know, some of the questions he had, I hope that there is that kind of dialogue that goes forth because this should be about trying to make sure there is not only a better day and a better change in our policy, but also a better day for the Cuban people.

So in that regard, and I have been down all of, been to Cuba several times and all other places in Latin America and the Caribbean, et cetera, and I have found that one of the major obstacles that we have had in the region is Cuba and our Cuban policy. It has caused a kind of friction, et cetera. They have all said to me that we needed to change. In fact, when I look at it, I think about multilateral relations as opposed to unilateral relations. We were the only country in the world, the only country in the world, all our major allies, everybody that had sanctions against Cuba, unlike, for example, this administration has been successful in putting together huge sanctions. When we work together, I think we are more successful. I think that is part of what has taken place, even Iran now with the P–5+1, even in Russia with the Russian sanctions. It is when we work closely with everyone. And I would like that to happen right here in our own hemisphere, but we need to work more closely with our allies.

Our closest and biggest allies, when I talked to them in Latin America, I asked what is the one thing that we should do in Latin America that would make it better for all of us that share this hemisphere? They said change our Cuban policy. Now, that being said, can we now, with the changing dynamics or with the new policy, after that, what realities with our allies and can we put additional pressure; or will they work with us to change and make human rights an issue high on their agenda so that we can make a difference in the lives of the people that are living on the island?

Ms. JACOBSON. Congressman, I think that is a critical point. And the next part of the question, we support your policy on Cuba. This is a very important day in Latin America, and for your relations with us, how can we help is, well, you can start raising the issue of human rights and democracy in Cuba much higher on your agenda. And we believe that this is going to be a very important turning point in countries' engagement, especially countries which have a history of working on these issues in the region that have been afraid to work with us too closely because of not wanting to appear aligned with our previous policy.

That has been evident in working on the summit where we were able to work strongly now with countries to highlight the democratic governance and citizens participation themes in the summit and accelerate planning on the civil society dialogue. It has been very evident even when I was in Cuba 2 weeks ago and we invited Ambassadors, not from this hemisphere—I spoke with them separately at one point—but we invited Ambassadors from Europe and Asia, for example, to a reception with dissidents and human rights activists. They never come to those receptions in the past, almost universally. There are few countries that have routinely come. They all came, and they were able to interact with dissidents for the first time. The dissidents had access to a wider range of diplomats than they had ever before. That is what we are hoping for.

Mr. MEEKS. Let me ask because I see I am running out of time, so I am going to ask two questions real, real quick. One, given that, and I know that there has been talk, has there been any real reactions directly from the Cuban civil society after the announcement? So I would like to know if there has been that, as well as, you know, when I was down there, one of the problems that I had was getting on the Internet. The Internet now will be open; and what, if any, impact would having an open Internet have on the civil society?

Ms. JACOBSON. Yeah. I mean, I think that would be huge. On Cuban civil society, I think the thing that struck me in both a small meeting with Cuban dissidents and then a much larger one, including many members, 12 members of the 57 who were released 4½ years ago are not able to travel. They are not permitted by the Cuban Government to travel, so I was able to see many of them. That has to change. They need to be able to travel.

But what I was struck by, I also met with El Critico, Angel Yunier, one of the younger members of this group. I was struck by the diversity of youth. Some support these measures and the change in policy, and some are obviously very strongly opposed, and I think that has to be respected, and we want to hear from and continue to support all of them.

The second thing is on the Internet, I think that is really crucial, and I don't know whether the Cuban Government will allow that opening. They have said they will. They have said they are interested in telecommunications. It is obviously critical to economic progress, but I think that is why we have to aggressively try and make it possible for our companies to provide that service and see whether the Cubans are willing, without the excuse that the Americans are the reason they can't do it.

Chairman ROYCE. We go now to Mr. Dana Rohrabacher of California.

Mr. ROHRABACHER. Thank you very much, Secretary Jacobson. This is a difficult task for you to be here. I think one of the main concerns that we have here is that instead of changing the Castro regime into a more democratic regime, the President is acting as if he has the right to rule by dictate and over his presidency is changing our country to be more like Castro than having Castro change to be more like a free and open society. Ruling by dictate and having secret negotiations is not what America is all about. That is not the way we make policy here, and many of us are very disappointed. This isn't the first case of this however, but dealing with a regime that is odorous—is "odorous" a word? Odorous, is that the word I want? There it is. Onerous and odorous. I think it is both. There you go. But we have a regime that stinks one way or the other and is oppressive one way or the other that we are dealing with, but yet we have had secret negotiations and deals that are announced to us, and you are here to explain it.

So let me ask this: When you said there are no concessions, you mean we go into an agreement with a regime, and we have had 50 years of American policy changed, and there are no concessions from the Cuban Government?

Ms. JACOBSON. I don't think there were concessions from the U.S. Government in going into——

Mr. ROHRABACHER. We have changed 50 years of American policy. Isn't that a concession enough? All right. Thank you. Let me ask you this; with the changes that we can expect, is there any agreement that part of this ending of U.S. policy, of making a stand that there be a more democratic and open society before we have a more expanded relationship with them, is there any agreement part of this that there will be, for example, independent unions, say we are going to have more economic activity? Was there any type of concession—well, the word "concessions." Is there an agreement that they are going to permit independent unions in Cuba?

Ms. JACOBSON. There were no agreements ahead of time on that.

Mr. ROHRABACHER. Okay. So we are going to open up economic trade. There are no unions, then we have also heard that maybe the money that is going into the pockets—supposedly into the pockets of the working people—is actually going to be transferred directly to the government; or that money might go directly to the government and then be handed out to the working people. Is that right? We agreed to that?

Ms. JACOBSON. We believe that on balance, the Cuban people will benefit more from this than the government will.

Mr. ROHRABACHER. That is not the question, whether you think it and whether we think it. Do you think the Cuban people want, that people who are going to be working for these companies that now we have permitted to go into Cuba, that the Cuban people want their government to take their pay and just give them back a pittance?

Ms. JACOBSON. I am sure they don't.

Mr. ROHRABACHER. Okay. Fine. Whose side are we on? On the side of the people who are taking the money from the central government. Are there going to be opposition parties, new opposition parties?

Ms. JACOBSON. We are going to continue to support those who want to have their voices heard peacefully——

Mr. ROHRABACHER. There have been no concessions on their part, so we have changed five decades of U.S. policy, and they still won't have any independent unions or opposition parties. I can't imagine that they are going to have opposition newspapers, and the rallies—listen, this is a regime. The Castro brothers came in, and once they were in power, they murdered the patriots who overthrew the Batista regime. They personally did. The fellow that we were negotiating with took a pistol and went and took these patriots out and shot them in the head by the hundreds. And after that, they decided to have a relationship with the Soviet Union, which

38

was then our main enemy, and encouraged the Soviet Union to put missiles that had nuclear weapons on them and encouraged them to use them on the United States. This is the regime we are dealing with, not to mention the criminals that they have given safe haven to. Now, how we can change five decades of policy by dictate from our President here? And then to hear there were no concessions on their side is disillusioning on our part and upsetting. Thank you very much.

Ms. ROS-LEHTINEN [presiding]. Thank you, Mr. Rohrabacher. And now we go to Mr. Sires of New Jersey.

Mr. SIRES. Thank you. Mr. Smith or Mr. Borman, can you tell me what percentage of the Cuban businesses are owned privately?

Mr. BORMAN. I can't tell you a precise percentage, but certainly there are over 200 categories of private sector economic activity that are authorized by the Cuban Government, so we recognize that it is——

Mr. SIRES. Authorized by the Cuban Government?

Mr. BORMAN. That they are legal, and there are private businesses.

Mr. SIRES. Mr. Smith, you?

Mr. SMITH. I don't have any additional details.

Mr. SIRES. I can tell you. About 15 percent. Eighty-five percent of the businesses in Cuba are owned by the military. The hotels are owned by the military. The bed and breakfasts are run by the families of the military. The umbrella agency that approves all the business is the son-in-law of one of the Castros. So when you say to me that the Cuban people, which is what I am interested in, are going to benefit by doing business with the Cuban people, you are not reaching very many people. You know, the private sector runs the hot dog stand, maybe. But we are talking about the big businesses which employs people are run by the generals. And if you want to put a big business in Cuba, you want to build a McDonald's and you need 100 employees, you have to go to the government, and you need 100 employees, you have to go to the government, and they give you the rate, and they give you the employees. And those employees are people who are part of the government system. So the people that are fighting for liberty and are fighting for democracy on the island are basically left out. These are the things you have to negotiate away from the Cuban Government.

So if your intention really is to help the Cuban people, the ordinary Cuban people, you are not helping them. This is a society that has upheld themselves with this kind of business that they run.

Mr. BORMAN. So just to be clear, the changes that we have made in our regulations are designed exactly to get items to the 15 percent. That is the way the regulations are structured so those items that can now be exported without individual licenses have to go to the true private sector.

Mr. SIRES. In terms of millions of dollars, Mr. Smith, this whole change, what do you think is going to benefit the Cuban Government, how many millions?

Mr. SMITH. We don't have a figure on any millions that would benefit the Cuban Government. I think the changes have been focused on private entrepreneurs, the small-scale business, private business that we are talking about. Again, I would repeat that most of the transactions between the United States and Cuba remain prohibited under these changes. We have just carved out a few areas that, as Mr. Borman talks about, are focused on the private entrepreneurs.

Mr. SIRES. I mean, if we go in to sell wheat to Cuba, are we going to buy sugar from Cuba? There is no real crop of sugar in Cuba anymore. Cuba used to be the leading world supplier of sugar. Cuba does business with the rest of the world. This whole idea that you have to grow this in some sort of a corporate has ruined the entire economy. There is no real free business in Cuba. Even the people that you deal with that you say they got 200 licenses, the Cuban Government can remove those license at a drop.

Ms. JACOBSON. It is true, Mr. Sires, but if I could, I met with seven or eight of these entrepreneurs, people really trying to run their own businesses, restaurateurs, a barber, women making soap, women doing decoration on clothes, and you can see people beginning to separate their own economic future from the government and having trouble because they can't get the supplies. The state doesn't want to provide them the supplies. That is who we are trying to help.

Mr. SIRES. But yet the elite in Cuba have all the supplies, and this is what I am trying to break. This is what runs the island, the generals, the people you see them driving in the cars. You see them living in the houses that were repossessed from people who worked hard in the business before the Castro takeover. I just don't see where we have any more leverage to get some of these changes to help the Cuban people.

I was just talking to my colleague. My aunt came from Cuba a couple years ago. I don't have a birth certificate. I asked her, when you go to Cuba, can you please get me a birth certificate. I don't know what my mother did with it. When she went to the municipal building what they said to her, we can't give you a birth certificate because we have him classified as a terrorist. I left at the age of 11, so I am a terrorist. And I don't want to share the story of what happened to my cousin who has a son who was educated in Russia to become an engineer. It is too tragic to even share that story with you because my feelings are that these people are just dictators. They are brutal dictators. People forget that Raul Castro, Che Guevara sent out the firing squads in Cuba that killed thousands of people, and I see people wearing a Che Guevara shirt. I am sorry. Thank you.

Ms. ROS-LEHTINEN. Thank you, Mr. Sires. Mr. Chabot, of Ohio.

Mr. CHABOT. Thank you, Madam Chairman, and thank you for calling this very important hearing to discuss the administration's new Cuba policy. I believe that President Obama's announcement to unilaterally change U.S. policy toward Cuba sets a dangerous precedent. In fact, it furthers an ongoing pattern of his utter disregard for Congress, but that is the way this administration operates. It gives a backhand to the elected representatives of the American people, and treats Congress like the proverbial mushrooms; keep them in the dark and feed them manure.

Ms. Jacobson, you said there were no concessions, and this wasn't necessarily something that the Cuban Government wanted. Those statements on their face, they are just not credible. You also said that the Obama administration was under no illusion about the nature of the Cuban Government. Well, I would submit that the administration is just about as naive about the nature of the Cuban Government, apparently as it was about ISIS when the President famously described them as the JV, or junior varsity. Tell that to the families of those who have been brutally massacred by those barbarians.

This Cuban policy, this new policy, is, in my view, tragically flawed. And the way it was brought about with such utter disregard—which you are hearing on both sides of the aisle—utter disregard for the elected Representatives of the American people, is disgraceful, and it is just as flawed.

Now, I would like to yield the balance of my time to the gentlelady from Florida, who as we all know was born in Cuba, and feels just as passionately about this as anybody in this place. Ileana Ros-Lehtinen.

Ms. ROS-LEHTINEN. Thank you so much, Mr. Chabot. And following up on your thought about the victims of brutality, wherever those victims are, I wanted to give Ms. Jacobson the opportunity, Assistant Secretary Jacobson, to answer the Alejandre family questions. How can Marlene Alejandre explain to her daughters why their grandfather who was killed by the Castro regime, his life meant nothing, and the person who was in jail as a co-conspirator for the murder of her father was pardoned, set free and returned to Cuba and received a hero's welcome. What does she say to her girls?

Ms. JACOBSON. Let me start out by saying I can never bring back her grandfather, and I can never do more than express my sadness and my condolences to her at the start. That is something that should not have happened.

Ms. ROS-LEHTINEN. When she was told by you and others that a trade would not take place, a trade by any other name—this was a swap, was it not? You talk about——

Ms. JACOBSON. Madam Chair, I just want to say an exchange of intelligence agents between two countries is something that this government and previous administrations have done many times.

Ms. ROS-LEHTINEN. But had the State Department not met with the family, and didn't the State Department time and time and time again tell her that Gerardo Hernandez would not be set free by this administration? Yes or no?

Ms. JACOBSON. To the best of my knowledge——

Ms. ROS-LEHTINEN. Did Secretary Kerry state right here to us that such a swap would not take place.

Ms. JACOBSON. That a swap for Alan Gross would not take place we affirmed and we did not do.

Ms. ROS-LEHTINEN. You just call it something else and say we were always telling the truth.

Ms. JACOBSON. We don't believe that is what took place.

Ms. ROS-LEHTINEN. Was the family under the impression, because you gave it to them, that that exchange would not take place, that Gerardo Hernandez would serve the complete sentence? Did you give that impression at any time or anyone in the State Department?

Ms. JACOBSON. Certainly I regret if the family felt additional pain because of an impression that we had left.

Ms. ROS-LEHTINEN. An impression, so that is all that they had to have. They had a false impression, that all this time while you were meeting with them, while you were meeting with them, you were already cooking up this swap, whatever you call it, that Gerardo Hernandez, for all intents and purposes, what happened is he was set free. He was pardoned by President Obama. He was returned to Cuba. He was given a hero's welcome, but that was just the impression that they got. It was a false impression because you were never going to do that. While you met with them. Don't you at least feel a little bit bad that you were lying to them?

Ms. JACOBSON. Well, in the first place, no one who met with the family ever lied to the family about what our understanding— Gerardo Hernandez was in jail on a lifetime——

Ms. ROS-LEHTINEN. My time is over. I am going to enjoy listening to the families when they hear that testimony coming from you. It is just pathetic. Thank you. Now Ms. Bass of California. Thank you, Mr. Chabot.

Ms. BASS. Thank you very much, Madam Chair. Let me just say before I begin, that this is, I find it particularly difficult to talk about Cuba because I want to acknowledge the experiences and the family situations of my colleagues, Mr. Sires, and also Ms. Ros-Lehtinen. But, you know, to talk about it and understand and acknowledge what your families went through, you know, I understand. I do, though, support what has happened in changing our relation with the island. And one of the things that I have always felt is that as an American, I want to be able to travel anywhere in the world, and I did recently go to Cuba specifically looking at a drug that the Cubans have invented for diabetes, and I want to talk about that in a minute. I have a couple of questions.

I know that this April there is the Summit of the Americas, and I wanted to know what the reaction has been from the international community about Cuba's participation, and other world leaders, regarding this policy change?

Ms. JACOBSON. Congresswoman, we have really seen universally from the hemisphere and those participating in the Summit that they strongly support the policy, that they think it changes the whole dynamic in the hemisphere for the United States on other objectives that we have, high priorities for us. It changes the entire debate. President Santos of Colombia called it historic. Dilma Rousseff said it changes the entire debate, President Rousseff of Brazil. They feel strongly that the policy of isolating Cuba was not the right one. We obviously disagreed with them for many years, but we found that it was isolating us in conversations and impeding our ability to have conversations on human rights and democracy not just in Cuba because they would not really engage on that issue, but also our ability to engage with them on human rights and democracy issues broadly speaking throughout the hemisphere, and we know that this is a concern in other countries in the hemisphere.

Ms. BASS. Okay. You know, about the trip that I mentioned that I recently took. It was the Congressional Diabetes Caucus went specifically because in Cuba they have developed a drug that is called Heberprot-P, and it basically is a drug that reduces the need for amputations in diabetics. As I understand, and I think my question is directed to Mr. Smith, as I understand, this drug has been approved for a clinical trial, but because of our policy it is not approved to be marketed in the U.S., which means that a company is not going to invest in a clinical trial if they can't market it. So I am wondering if the changes that have been made in the law would allow for this. And basically what the Cubans are reporting, but we obviously have to test it and see if it is correct, they have been able to reduce the need for amputations by 70 percent, and we have tens of thousands of people in the United States who are diabetics who wind up losing their limbs, their feet, because of diabetes. Are you aware of what I am talking about?

Mr. Smith. Madam, I am. Nothing in the recent changes changes our policy with respect to those types of drugs. But they are not prohibited from coming into the United States flat out. Those companies can apply to OFAC for a specific license. We have a long history of evaluating those license applications. We receive them. We refer them to other agencies in the United States Government, including the State Department and often the Food and Drug Administration. And we evaluate whether any additional U.S. activity with respect to those drugs makes sense. And then we can grant what is called a specific license to authorize it.

Ms. Bass. The other pressure that I feel coming from California is from the agricultural industries, and I am wondering if the policy changes would lead to our ability to export. There is a number of companies in California that are interested in exporting agricultural goods as well as livestock.

Mr. Smith. So what we have heard over time is that, even though there are certain categories of transactions and goods that have been authorized, including agricultural products, we have heard from exporters and many Members of Congress that our previous financing rules didn't help the situation and didn't help them to be competitive with their counterparts in other countries. So what we did is, we made a change to provisions in a statute that deals with the term "cash in advance," and basically we have made it more advantageous for U.S. exporters to export their products. This is what they have been asking for—to make them more competitive—and what many Members of Congress have been asking us to do.

Ms. Bass. Thank you.

Ms. Ros-Lehtinen. Thank you so much, Ms. Bass. And we will go to Judge Poe of Texas.

Mr. Poe. Let me start with the presumption that Cuba is a violator of human rights. I think we all know that, especially the folks in Cuba. The policy of the President, I think, I don't want to go into the issue of whether, with or without Congress' approval, the President made some decisions. I want to cut to the one issue that I have a question about. What is the purpose of the current U.S. policy toward Cuba? That we basically have no contact with them. We don't trade with them generally. This policy that we have been talking about that has been implemented for 50-something years, what is the purpose? What is the goal of that policy? Is that clear?

Ms. Jacobson. You mean the previous policy?

Mr. POE. Well, the previous policy until it was changed by this President, tweaked a little bit.

Ms. JACOBSON. The goal of the previous policy was that via isolation of Cuba and keeping our distance from that government, we would hope to bring about change in the regime and simultaneously we would hope to empower the Cuban people to be able to make that change.

Mr. POE. Change the regime? Change their communism? Change what?

Ms. JACOBSON. Certainly change their behavior toward their own citizens.

Mr. POE. So our goal is that Cuba internally changes the treatment of Cuban citizens? I am not trying to catch you on semantics. I am just trying to see what our goal is. Our goal is to do this so that the Cuban people are treated like they should be?

Ms. JACOBSON. In terms of international human rights standards and that sort of thing, yes.

Mr. POE. And would you say that has not worked?

Ms. JACOBSON. I would.

Mr. POE. Fifty years doing something and if it doesn't change, that policy or that goal has not been achieved because the Cubans are treated, I think, just as bad as they ever have been.

Ms. JACOBSON. I believe so, yes, sir.

Mr. POE. Let me ask you this: Is the policy, is our goal ever to do what—our relationship with Cuba, whatever that may be in the future. Is that for America's benefit or for Cuba's benefit? As we look at changes toward Cuba, is this because we want to help American businesses, for example, or Americans to be able to travel; is that the goal that we are moving toward, or are we looking to a goal of what is still best for the Cubans?

Ms. JACOBSON. Our goal is to do what is in our national interest and to help the Cuban people to be able to do what they wish, to be able to make their own decisions.

Mr. POE. So it is both?

Ms. JACOBSON. Yes. I would say the first priority is to do what is in our national interest, which includes our core values of democracy and universal human rights.

Mr. POE. Would our policy have anything to do with helping trade from the United States?

Ms. JACOBSON. Certainly.

Mr. POE. Let me give you an example. I am from Texas. I represent a lot of, not as many as I used to, but a lot of rice farmers. When I got elected to Congress, I thought rice came in a box. I have learned a lot about rice farming. There is long grain; there is short grain; there is two seasons, all that stuff. Historically, Texas rice farmers traded internationally with Iran, Iraq, and Cuba. Bummer. You can see that that hasn't worked out so well. They want to trade long grain rice to Cuba. The Cubans want to buy long grain rice. They want that as opposed to California short grain rice. Well, they do. Set aside all the other issues. Would that not be in the best interests of the United States and American exporters that we would facilitate trade with Cuba?

Ms. JACOBSON. You are going to get me into some trouble because I am not sure I can set aside all the other issues, but if I really could in a vacuum, it would be in our interests. I am not sure we always do those things in a vacuum, though.

Mr. POE. Oh, I understand that. There is a lot of other issues to be involved. What I am saying is having this barrier, to me, of trade hurts Americans. I don't know about the Cubans. They get their rice from Vietnam. Oh, I am out of time. I have some other questions that I would like to submit for the record to be answered.

Mr. ROS-LEHTINEN. Without objection.

Mr. POE. Thank you very much.

Ms. ROS-LEHTINEN. Thank you, Judge Poe. And we will go to Mr. Cicilline of Rhode Island.

Mr. CICILLINE. Thank you, Madam Chair, and thank you to the witnesses. I too want to begin by acknowledging the experiences and passionate leadership on Cuba-American relations by Chairwoman Ros-Lehtinen and Mr. Sires, and thank you for being so open with your experiences at this committee. I think it adds to our understanding of these really complicated issues.

I think all members of this committee are equally and deeply committed to help the Cuban people achieve freedom and democracy, and I think the difference of opinion is what is the best strategy for bringing that about, and I really thank the witnesses for being here today, and I expect that you will continue to keep Congress informed throughout these discussions with the Cuban Government. And I am hopeful, and I think most Americans are hopeful that the President's efforts to engage in real and substantive negotiations with the Cuban Government will ultimately advance the national security interests of the United States and benefit the Cuban people. But I think like most Americans, I remain very deeply concerned about the long record of human rights abuses and the denial of basic freedoms that have been caused at the hands of the Cuban dictatorship. And while our current policy has failed to bring about lasting change in Cuba, as we update our policy, I think we have to be sure that we are doing it in a measured, comprehensive, and thoughtful way that is aligned with the current reality. My hope is that the President's efforts here are met with honest engagement by the Cuban Government toward a more open, free, and tolerant society for the Cuban people.

So my questions really are, I have really three questions, and I invite you to respond to them. The first is, there has been a lot of talk about what the neighbors and our allies in the region have for a long time identified as a problem, the Cuba-U.S. policy. So what is really the kind of best way that we can engage some of these partners in the region who now can point to a change in policy to really use them in a way to help bring about the kind of liberties and democracy in Cuba that we all want? What's the strategy for effectively engaging others in the region to be partners in this work now that the policy has begun to change? The second is, how can we as a Congress best advance this issue of human rights which continues to be a very, very serious issue in a variety of different ways? How do we play a role enforcing real progress and helping establish progress on the human rights issue?

And, finally, to build on Mr. Sires' question, how do we ensure that this economic engagement that is intended here, which is, of course, intended to support the Cuban people, does not instead fortify the government at a particularly critical time? How do we protect against an unintended consequence where we think we are helping entrepreneurs in the private sector strengthen, but at the same time are, in fact, helping the government at a moment when others are beginning to retract some of their support? I invite you to respond to those questions, please.

Ms. JACOBSON. Thank you. A couple of things. On engaging our allies, there is a couple of thoughts I have about that. One is that all of the countries in the region, as well as our European allies and others, have Embassies on the island. Many of them were hesitant, if not outright refused to engage with many of the democracy activists for years. I am very optimistic if not having seen concrete results already that they have lost that fear with our change of policy. I think that is hugely important. Their rhetoric outside the country is important in dialogues, but engaging with these activists and supporting them on the island I think is just as important. These people are often accused of being our tools. I think that others need to embrace them openly and talk to them, work with them, engage with them, hear from them, and we are saying that to them.

The other thing is in terms of Congress, I hope as many as possible will have real congressional delegations that will go to the island and see as many in Cuban civil society, and that includes in the arts, in the democracy area, as well as entrepreneurs and hear from the ones I heard from, how they are trying to keep those funds from going to the Cuban Government, but how they believe they are making their own way independently even if some of those funds are going to the Cuban Government, because I think the psychology of those entrepreneurs is a breaking away from the state that is worth that price. The Cuban Government went through the period of decline of the Soviet Union where it dropped GDP by 30 percent, and they survived, so I think this is important that we support those efforts.

Ms. ROS-LEHTINEN. Thank you so much, Mr. Cicilline.

Mr. CICILLINE. I yield back. Thank you.

Ms. ROS-LEHTINEN. And we turn to Mr. Salmon of Arizona.

Mr. SALMON. Thank you. Ms. Jacobson, when specifically—I am looking for a date—did you find out about the White House-Cuba negotiations and the content of the President's announcement?

Ms. JACOBSON. What I can tell you, Representative Salmon, is that I was aware from throughout that the Embassy of the White House was undertaking efforts to secure the release of Alan Gross because we were working on the Gross case with the family.

Mr. SALMON. I understand that, but when did you find out specifically about the negotiations that have been going on for the past year? What date did you find out about those?

Ms. JACOBSON. It was about 6 weeks or 2 months before the announcement that I knew more of the content of those discussions.

Mr. SALMON. Okay. And when did you find out about the announcement itself?

Ms. JACOBSON. When the actual date of the announcement was decided, I knew about it.

Mr. SALMON. You found out simultaneously with the announcement being made?

Ms. JACOBSON. No, no, no, no, no. As that was being decided, I knew about that. In other words, I knew about the decision to announce the new policy about 6 weeks as it was being decided before, and so the date of the announcement I knew about as that was being decided at the White House.

Mr. SALMON. Okay. Can you tell me what resources, what U.S. resources were used to ensure that Gerardo Hernandez, convicted of killing four U.S. citizens and a member of the Cuban 5, could artificially inseminate his wife? What resources were used for that?

Ms. JACOBSON. What I can tell you on that is that we have always, the State Department, from my perspective, have always facilitated the visits of his wife to the prison in California when he was incarcerated.

Mr. SALMON. Right.

Ms. JACOBSON. So those were the resources that we expended in terms of her visit.

Mr. SALMON. I understand that he was able to artificially inseminate his wife, and that was facilitated by the U.S. Government.

Ms. JACOBSON. Beyond our efforts to facilitate her visits, the rest was done by the Department of Justice, and I would have to defer to the Department of Justice.

Mr. SALMON. I would like to know that. I think it is incredulous that it would be a U.S. priority to make sure Hernandez fathered a child while he was in incarceration, so I will wait for an answer on that.

Last question, these secret negotiations went on for over a year and reportedly consisted of seven meetings, so when you went to Havana last month for talks, the Cubans made it very, very clear they would not allow our diplomats to speak to dissidents, and normalization was not possible without the return of our Naval base in Guantanamo Bay, as well as other nonstarters that we have talked about today. So what did we really accomplish, other than maybe getting a T-shirt that I have had meetings for over a year and all I got was this lousy T-shirt?

Ms. JACOBSON. Well, I guess I would start out by saying we got an intelligence asset out of Cuba who was languishing in jail there, and we got Alan Gross home, and you know that. But beyond that, the beginning of this process of normalization starts with diplomatic relations, which is only the first start. Normalization is going to take years, and we made it very clear that it includes things like property claims, which has to be part of this discussion, judgments against the Cuban Government, which have been adjudicated in U.S. courts which has to be part of this. So that is a much longer process, and we haven't acceded to any of the things——

Mr. SALMON. No, and I don't expect that we will acquiesce to any of——

Ms. JACOBSON. It is the start of the process.

Mr. SALMON. I understand, but what was your response when they said we are not going to do anything on normalization until you do these things?

Ms. JACOBSON. Well, but what they meant by normalization is the end of that year's long process, not restoration of diplomatic relations, which is the first part. So I am presuming that they mean they won't have full normalization until all those things are done, but they will have a restoration of diplomatic relations.

Mr. SALMON. Thanks. I yield back.

Ms. ROS-LEHTINEN. Thank you very much, sir. Mr. Connolly of Virginia is recognized.

Mr. CONNOLLY. I thank the chair. Ms. Jacobson, I believe in politics and in diplomacy in a very simple adage, don't give it away for nothing. I am very troubled by the abrupt change in U.S. policy to Cuba at precisely a moment where we actually have leverage. For 50 years, one could argue the Castro brothers have loved U.S. policy because it has helped keep them in power. Fair enough. But that was then. This is now. Things have changed. They are hurting. The economy is hurting. Their oil supplier is hurting. And as they look out to the future, it is very difficult to see a viable Cuban economy without major change, including a change in the relationship with us.

Now, I take your point about diplomatic exchange, and I put that aside, but the liberalization in trade and tourism and investment, and, indeed, the President has called to begin the process of dismantling the embargo that has been in place for half a century. I need to understand what we got in return? Where is the reciprocity? Why wouldn't the United States use its good offices and its leverage with respect to human rights, with respect to press freedoms, with respect to religious freedoms, with respect to political dissidents. In our briefings from State Department personnel, the answer we got when we asked that question was we are not doing that. To me, I must admit, that is shocking and I think a disappointment to many that we wouldn't use the leverage we finally had to some good point. And I wonder if you would address that, because I think we have squandered leverage.

Ms. JACOBSON. First I want to start out by saying that what liberalization there has been in regulations, and my colleagues would certainly specify on all this, is very specific, and I think Mr. Smith has repeatedly noted that most transactions still remain prohibited.

Mr. CONNOLLY. If I may, fair enough, but the promise of the President, he said explicitly, we are going to start the process of dismantling the embargo. So Cubans see promise, not just here and now, but a pathway toward the dismantlement of a policy we have had in place for a half a century.

Ms. JACOBSON. And the President said he would like to see the debate over that. There is no doubt. But the Cubans keep demanding this in part because it is still there, so they know that this is not a big liberalization yet.

In addition, I think the most important thing that we have made clear to them is we are not letting up on human rights. If you were to try and be transactional about this with the Cuban Government, the problem with that is that they won't trade for anything, and we will end up still not helping the Cuban people. The goal of these policies is not to do something that relies on the Cuban Government agreeing to give us something for a human rights concession. We want to try and go directly to the Cuban people. Now, it is true, they may not let the telecommunications companies work for more Internet access, but what has been news all over Cuba and every

Cuban knows, is that we are restarting our relations, and the bogeyman of the U.S. being their problem is no longer credible.

Mr. CONNOLLY. Again, my time is limited. I appreciate that, and I wouldn't deny that there are lots of people who see lots of hope in what has now been started. But my question is really more specific. What is the reciprocity? What did we get out of this other than the aspirations that things will get better with this change because they weren't getting better under the old regime? I can't think of a single thing—the release of Mr. Gross, of course—but in terms of a policy shift, a concession, I can't think of a single one you have announced.

Ms. JACOBSON. I believe that we also will get some things that matter in opening our Embassy and hopefully the ability to travel throughout the country and see more people and support more people. We can't really move outside Havana right now.

Mr. CONNOLLY. That is what you hope to negotiate.

Ms. JACOBSON. But that is necessary for opening an Embassy. That is part of this. I also think that, you know, we will have all of these dialogues that they want to have for cooperation, that will be part of those discussions as well. It is to come. I agree.

Mr. CONNOLLY. Madam Chairman, I know my time is up, but I want to underline, I always think it is a mistake in foreign policy to give it away for nothing.

Ms. ROS-LEHTINEN. Thank you, Mr. Connolly, and now we turn to Mr. Duncan, the chairman of our Subcommittee on the Western Hemisphere.

Mr. DUNCAN. Thank you, Madam Chairman.

You know, if trade and lifting the sanctions is seen as a cure-all of foreign policy for the Obama administration with regard to oppressive regimes like Cuba, then why did the administration impose more sanctions on Venezuela the very same week as the policy shift in Cuba? Is this an indication that we may see similar normalized relations with North Korea, Venezuela or other oppressive regimes?

Ms. JACOBSON. The sanctions that were imposed on Venezuela this past week were, in fact, additional visa sanctions. We——

Mr. DUNCAN. In December, the same week as the President started normalizing relations with Cuba he imposed some sanctions on Venezuela.

Ms. JACOBSON. If you are talking about the signing of the legislation that was passed by Congress, that includes both visa sanctions and assets freezes. It is not a trade sanction bill.

Mr. DUNCAN. Are we going to see any more normalizations? Are there going to be other surprises? We didn't see Cuba coming. What are we going to do with Venezuela, North Korea or any of the others? Are you anticipating any of that?

Ms. JACOBSON. I can't speak outside my region, but I don't expect you to see any surprises on Venezuela. We have been consulting on that, and I expect to continue, nor any surprises on Cuba. We will continue to consult on that.

Mr. DUNCAN. I think you were surprised over the Cuba talks and you weren't brought in or read into it until late in the discussions, but let's move on because many of the people that I speak with about this policy shift on Cuba, some even here in Congress, talk about, and point to, the freedom now afforded Americans to travel to Cuba.

So what I ask is, is the same freedom of travel a two-way street? Is the same freedom of travel afforded to the Cuban people to travel to the United States? In this policy shift, all American travelers really stay, unless it is family travel, they stay at hotels owned by the Cuban military. Only state-owned enterprises can accept credit cards. Article 18 of the Cuban constitution requires all foreign commerce to be controlled by the state. So how does increasing commerce with Castro's monopolies help the Cuban people?

Ms. JACOBSON. Let me start out by saying on travel by Cubans, we are looking at that really carefully. Since the 2013 decision by the Cuban Government to allow more people to travel, it has gotten better. You have been able to have some dissidents here to speak in front of this House who have never been able to before, but it is, by far, not good enough. There are still people who can't travel, and they should be able to. They should all be able to travel freely.

Let me say that on the trade portion, I will go back to what I said. We understand that there will be some benefits to the Cuban Government. We really do believe, again, because of people that we have talked to who are entrepreneurs, because of activists, because of artists, because of some of the small agricultural folks working, that they will benefit more than the government will if we are able to implement these regulations and get them the equipment they need that the government won't provide them.

Mr. DUNCAN. Right. They will benefit from maybe some economic transaction. I will give you that. We will see.

How about other freedoms for the Cuban people? What was negotiated in this? Freedom of speech? Freedom of religion? Economic freedom? Freedom of assembly and protest? And I point to Ms. Berta Soler's testimony yesterday. I think Chris Smith talked about it, but she said,

> "The truth is the Government of Cuba represses our right to freedom of religion and association, and so we go out, participate in religious activities on Sundays and then are detained. The government is constantly repressing activists who are trying to gather together to discuss issues that are important to them."

So the right to peacefully assemble and protest against a repressive government is still there. So I ask this: What did the U.S. barter in exchange for this new policy shift other than Alan Gross' release that benefits the Cuban people and ultimately gives them more freedoms? I mean, that is what I am about. I want this to be about the Cuban people. If we are truly going to pursue a policy to normalize relations, it ought to be about the Cuban people and not the Castro regime, and the Castro regime is the only one that I see that benefits from this economically through the businesses they own and operate. I don't see where private property rights are really going to—you know, maybe. You mentioned that earlier. I think somebody asked that question, but private property rights and the claims by American Cubans—Cuban Americans and Cuban people in general that own property that was nationalized by the Federal Government.

How are we going to address that? I think the private property rights is so important and is sort of left out of this discussion, and you and I talked about this in my office the other day. I think that is critical. So I would like you to you talk about the freedoms for the American people—I mean, the Cuban people—in the remaining 20 seconds that I have.

Ms. JACOBSON. Thank you, Mr. Chairman, and I agree with you that all of those things are what we are seeking as an end. I think we all agree that is the goal here.

Mr. DUNCAN. So tell me how this policy gets us to that goal?

Ms. JACOBSON. The policy gets us to this goal, number one, by having a lot more people able to work with us on it from outside Cuba than ever before. We were alone. We were not joined by anyone else. We are more effective with allies. Number two, we believe that there were no concessions here. Some of these things are things that we are doing that deeply worry the Cuban Government because they may not be able to control them, and we don't believe that anything we did on December 17th, as the President and the Secretary have said, were concessions to the government.

Mr. DUNCAN. Well my time is up, but the concessions for the Cuban people are important, and I yield back.

Ms. ROS-LEHTINEN. Thank you so much.

I will now yield to Mr. Lowenthal of California.

Mr. LOWENTHAL. Thank you, Madam Chair, and I would like to preface my remarks by saying that I have been touched listening to both the experiences of those that have been the most affected by the repressive regime, and that has been—I join with Congressman Cicilline and Congresswoman Bass in saying that I have been touched by the testimony of both Congressman Sires and Ros-Lehtinen, who talk about their families and some of the impacts.

But having said that, I am very supportive of our re-engagement and the restoration of diplomatic relations. I say that not because I support many of the repressive issues that take place, but I say that as someone who represents one of the largest if not the largest Vietnamese American communities in the United States, people who escaped also an intolerable situation, who I believe, while certainly very, very against the existing regime in Vietnam, have benefited by having, I think, greater ability to communicate some of their concerns, and they have had it by having the U.S. Ambassador to Vietnam come to a community which is not at all supportive of that government and really have a dialogue and be able to express some of their concerns. I see that as a very, very positive step.

So my questions are, as we go forward, will there be a strategy also to reach out to the Cuban American community in the United States who have been suffering a great deal and who have the relatives? So that is my first question.

Ms. JACOBSON. Absolutely. Absolutely, sir. And we have begun to do that knowing that the views in that community are diverse as well, and seeing that activists within Cuba, among the four points they could agree on, was that the Cuban Diaspora has to be taken into consideration.

Mr. LOWENTHAL. I think that is so important, and I really—if anyone else wants—I really think that is very important, and I also would like to know what people have—what we see as—as we move forward there is more trade and more tourism, how are we going to deal with—when many of those tourists go back to Cuba and speak out against their government that is in Cuba, have we talked some of those issues?

Ms. JACOBSON. We certainly considered that in terms of Cubans coming to the United States, and when that travel policy was liberalized, there was an enormous concern among activists that if they left and spoke freely, they either wouldn't be able to go home, perhaps, or if they went home, they would never be able to travel again.

The fact that some of them have now been able to travel repeatedly, I think, is a good sign, but everyone still is fearful.

Mr. LOWENTHAL. As I am, and so with that I——

Ms. JACOBSON. And we raised that issue.

Mr. LOWENTHAL. Does anyone else have any issues or want to respond to any—some of the issues—as the policies begin to change, what you see in the future as some of the consequences. Not so much the reasons—I am wanting to move forward. Where do we go from here? What do you see things that we need to look at as this policy has changed now?

Mr. BORMAN. Well, the two points I would make is, one, we certainly, with the Treasury, are doing a lot of outreach to all segments of the American public so they understand what the current—the new changes are; and then, secondly, we will be watching very carefully to see how they actually play out in practice, because coming back to the 15 percent of the Cuban population or the Cuban economy that is private sector, we are really looking to strengthen and grow that with these opportunities. So that is something we will certainly be looking at very carefully.

Mr. SMITH. I would echo those comments. I think the implementation is what we are going to be looking at over the next few months, and years, actually, and to see what the effects are and what we need to do to make these——

Mr. LOWENTHAL. As a member also, because of my own concerns and also because of the concerns of the communities I represent, I have joined—I have been a very active member of the Tom Lantos Human Rights Commission. I have adopted prisoners of conscience in Vietnam, actually put pressure on the Vietnamese Government to begin to release some of these prisoners. I would like to see some of the same efforts even be increased as we go forward with our changed policy in Cuba.

And thank you, and I yield back.

Ms. ROS-LEHTINEN. Thank you, Mr. Lowenthal, and we go to Mr. Brooks of Alabama.

Mr. BROOKS. Thank you, Madam Chairman.

I believe that America's policies should be consistent throughout the globe as best that we can do so, and by way of example, I would like to just make a quick comparison between Cuba and Saudi Arabia, looking at some of this similarities between the countries, some of the differences, and also the disparate ways in which each is treated by the United States Government.

On trade, American/Cuban trade is very limited, as we all know. Less than $500 million per year in exports by America to Cuba.

But America/Saudi trade is very robust. Roughly $80 billion per year, perhaps higher.

On travel, travel to Cuba, very limited by the United States Government. Saudi Arabia, quite the opposite.

On Embassies and diplomatic interaction, in Saudi Arabia we have an Embassy and very significant diplomatic interaction. In Cuba, we have no Embassy and little to no diplomatic interaction.

I could go on and on, but I think it is fair to say that the United States treats Cuba substantially differently than Saudi Arabia.

As I have listened to the witnesses and member comments concerning Cuba and why Cuba must be treated differently, I can't help but emphasize some of the similarities and differences that have been pointed out.

On the issue of freedom of religion, as bad as Cuba may be, and we have heard some comments as to how bad it is, the question is, is Saudi Arabia worse? One member commented that some religious observance requires Cuba Government consent. Yet in Saudi Arabia, open worship by Christians is a criminal offense, as is missionary work. If a Muslim dares question whether Islam is a true religion, he is severely punished. Raef Badawi being a recent example, facing 1,000 lashes and 6 to 10 years in prison, assuming, of course, that the lashing does not kill him.

On the issue of dictatorial governments, one would again be hard-pressed to determine which family government, that of Cuba's or the Saudi's is more dictatorial. I think you could have a very robust debate concerning that issue.

On the issue of terrorism, bearing in mind that 15 of the 19 9/11 terrorists were Saudis, and also bearing in mind that so much terrorism funding originates in Saudi Arabia, in fairness, much of it opposed by the Riyadh regime, but, nonetheless, still a lot of money for terrorism comes from the country of Saudi Arabia, one could have a lively debate again concerning which country poses a greater threat to world peace.

Given so many similarities, and also some differences, but with Saudi Arabia being treated so much better by the United States of America, what factors, in your mind, justify treating Cuba so much worse than Saudi Arabia that supports the 50-year policy that the United States has had with respect to Cuba?

Ms. JACOBSON. Thank you, Congressman. I think that our own view has been pretty clearly laid out by the President on the 17th, and the Secretary certainly made a number of comments that we believe that Cuba, not on its merits necessarily in terms of its behavior, but on the effectiveness of policy argument, the efficiency and what is in our national interest, merits a change in that policy, and so it was announced in December.

I can't necessarily make that comparison between Saudi Arabia and Cuba, but I will say that we believe very strongly that the values and the ideals of the United States need to be pursued aggressively all over, the world, and that they are best pursued, and you could expect this from a diplomat at the State Department via diplomatic relations and having Embassies. Those aren't concessions or gifts. We do them effectively when we have a presence, and that is why we want to have that presence in Cuba.

Mr. BROOKS. I am running short of time. Let me ask this final question.

Americais always faced with a very difficult choice. On the one hand, we can be open, hoping that our relations with this country will slowly but surely cause them to accept freedoms that we cherish in America, or we can be very restrictive, as we have been with Cuba, North Korea, and some other nations, in hopes that the punishment will be sufficient.

What do you think long term is best for Cuba?

Ms. JACOBSON. I think we are most effective when we have allies with us, and we were alone vis-à-vis Cuba. So I believe the openness with allies to the Cuban people, not the Cuba Government, will be effective.

Ms. ROS-LEHTINEN. Gentleman's time is expired.

Mr. Deutch of Florida is recognized.

Mr. DEUTCH. Thank you, Madam Chairman and Ranking Member Engel for working so quickly to ensure that this committee was able to hear from the administration on the policy shift.

I represent South Florida where the administration's announcement has a tremendous impact, and let me first say that in the immediate term, I have serious concerns about the Castro regime's continuing human rights abuses, as many of my colleagues have brought up today, and I hope that we expect and demand more of them.

Coinciding with the administration's announcement, one of the major South Florida's newspapers, The Sun Sentinel, published an in-depth feature called Plundering America, which exposed the way in which underground criminal networks have exploited U.S. policy toward Cuba.

Madam Chairman, the United States opened its doors to the Cuban people so they could have a better life free from the oppressive Castro regime, and the overwhelming majority of those who have come here have made incredible contributions to this country and become a deep part of the fabric of our society. What great examples we have here on this panel with our colleagues and my friends, Chairman Emeritus Ros-Lehtinen and Representative Sires, but policies that were put in place to ensure that those who sought refuge in the U.S. would still be able to see their families or send remittances are being taken advantage of by a small minority for criminal gain. Individuals engaged in organized criminal activity have turned our humanitarian policy into an underground criminal enterprise by using their ability to return to and from Cuba to engage in illicit fraud activities, particularly, the report noted, Medicare fraud, and are transporting large sums of cash back to the island and evading arrest as the Cuban regime will not extradite these fugitives.

As The Sun Sentinel notes, they have turned our open-door policy into a revolving door, enabling, and I quote, ''Crooks from the island to rob American businesses and taxpayers of more than $2 billion over two decades.''

As the administration rebalances its relationship with Cuba, I hope we are not ignoring the years of criminal activity that the Castros have turned a blind eye to, at best. We need to know what extent—to what extent the regime or people connected to the regime have been or will continue to be involved in these illegal crime rings.

Assistant Secretary Jacobson, I would like to know if your initial round of talks with the Cubans included any discussion of extradition of fugitives from Cuba; and if not, when and how will this issue be raised?

Ms. JACOBSON. Thank you, Congressman, and it certainly did include the discussion of fugitives. It did not specifically include the question of extradition. As you know, we have a very old extradition treaty that has not been used in many years. I have no idea whether we will get back eventually to actually using it. But it certainly included the question of fugitives and the desire to have much more in-depth conversation about law enforcement and fugitive issues in the future.

Mr. DEUTCH. Can you just elaborate a bit on the extradition you referred to, the situation that we have now, but in the talks——

Ms. JACOBSON. Right. Let me——

Mr. DEUTCH [continuing]. How did the talks focus on that?

Ms. JACOBSON. I just want to be clear that the morning of the talks that I had were on the diplomatic restoration. The afternoon of the talks were on a whole series of subjects on which we are going to have experts, who are not me, have much more substantive conversations about what we want, right, and that is one of the subjects.

Mr. DEUTCH. And when—what will be the context of those discussions and when will they take place?

Ms. JACOBSON. Right. We are going to try and set those up as quickly as possible. Part of that conversation already began in the migration talks, because we take with us our lawyers and the Department of Justice, and we talk about fugitives in the context of the migration talks. So we have actually begun that one, but we will have a separate conversation on law enforcement and fugitives, basically, as we can set these up in the time schedule.

The Cubans are a little bit overwhelmed by our new wanting to have dialogues on lots of different subjects. They have accepted the idea of having that, and we will get them set up as soon as we can with our Justice Department colleagues.

Mr. DEUTCH. Thank you.

Mr. Smith, understanding that much of this falls under law enforcement agencies' purview, has your office looked at where the money coming from these Cuban criminal networks—where all of that money, which usually comes back to Cuba in cash goes, or the role of Cuban Government in sponsoring or even training these individuals or what is being done to impede their activities?

Mr. SMITH. OFAC does work with our law enforcement colleagues on a variety of issues that relate to sanctions.

With respect to any particular issues with regard to money flows or anything that might impact the U.S. law or U.S. sanctions, I couldn't talk about anything that we would actually be looking at.

Mr. DEUTCH. Can you speak to the specific situation that was described at great length in these newspaper reports?

Mr. SMITH. I think most of what you described at great length from the newspaper reports and the details from the newspaper reports, I would refer to the Department of Justice. I think that they would have the primary equities there and the primary statutes that would be involved.

What we would do at OFAC is, we enforce the sanctions laws, and very little, from what I have seen, would impact our regulations that we would enforce.

Mr. DEUTCH. Thank you.

Thank you, Madam——

Ms. ROS-LEHTINEN. Thank you. Gentleman's time has expired.

Mr. DeSantis of Florida.

Mr. DESANTIS. Thank you, Madam Chairman.

Secretary Jacobson, you said in response to Chairman Royce's question what we did not make concessions to the Cuban Government, but yet later in your answers you have conceded that the increased economic activity will have some benefit to the Cuban Government. So that is a concession. Is it not?

Ms. JACOBSON. It is a benefit they may receive.

Mr. DESANTIS. Especially given their two main patrons, Venezuela and Russia, they are reeling with a change in world oil prices, and I think the Castro government very much wants any type of patronage they can get, and I think as Mr. Sires pointed out, you know, money that goes into that country is going to be controlled by the government, and if you are going to argue differently, why is it that we are really the only country that has these restrictions. So you have open relations, Switzerland, Australia, whoever. How come with all those ties, the Cuban people have not benefited, because you said in your testimony in response to a question of Mr. Poe that the Cuban people are not better off after 50 years of our policy.

My question is if the other policies of all the other countries in the world are so good, why haven't the Cuban people benefited from those policies?

Ms. JACOBSON. Congressman, I think part of the problem in terms of actual sort of economic policy in Cuba is that they have not modernized their system, opened their system, made a foreign investment law that adequately attracts investment to have those other countries be part of it.

Mr. DESANTIS. And they said that they are not going to change. Raul Castro said they are not changing. He said this is a victory for the Cuban revolution, and we are not going to change. So I don't see where you get that the people of Cuba are somehow going to benefit more than the regime. I think the regime will benefit from this, but until there is a change, I think the benefits are going to be bottled up at the top.

Ms. JACOBSON. But remittances also go directly to Cuban people. We raised the remittance amounts, in addition. One of the reasons that they haven't rushed to us to implement the telecommunications provisions or the Internet provisions, you know, they have been very, very wary of all of this is because they know full well that they probably won't be able to control it, and that the benefits may well reach the Cuban people.

Mr. DESANTIS. And so they are probably not likely to do—let me ask you this: When you took your trip, were you given access to any of the places where political prisoners are being held, view that?

Ms. JACOBSON. I was not.

Mr. DESANTIS. Okay. Is there any discussion—has the administration trying to get property returned that was confiscated both of American citizens when Castro took power, including Cuban Americans who were exiled?

Ms. JACOBSON. We made clear in the conversations that the issue of expropriated properties has to be part of normalization.

Mr. DESANTIS. What was their response?

Ms. JACOBSON. They agreed that that has to be part of the conversation and responded that they had issues they wanted to raise with us about losses under the embargo.

Mr. DESANTIS. And one of the issues, I know they wanted is GTMO. Can you categorically state that on January 20th, 2017, at 12 o'clock p.m., a date that a lot of my constituents are looking forward to, that GTMO will still be under U.S. control, the Naval base?

Ms. JACOBSON. I am certain that Guantanamo will still be a U.S. base, but I can't tell you a hypothetical about what may be part of these normalization talks. But it is not on the table for us right now, and I don't envision that, but I am not a high enough ranking person to know, and it is—I am not from the Department of Defense. Et cetera, to know whether it could be in the future, and—but I can't——

Mr. DESANTIS. Well, I am just talking about over the next 2 years as this administration is in power, but I understand it is not going to be——

Ms. JACOBSON. I can't envision that.

Mr. DESANTIS. Cuba is a state sponsor of terrorism. The Federal statutes, in order to be removed from that list, there are certain criteria. One of them is that the government has to provide assurances that they will not support international terrorism.

Has the Cuban Government provided those assurances, and if so, are they credible?

Ms. JACOBSON. Cuba has repeatedly rejected international terrorism, and we are in the process right now as we review this of also looking at their statements and evaluating whether they have or whether they will give such assurances.

Mr. DESANTIS. Well, I am concerned, because if they say they are not going to change, they have been a state sponsor of terrorism. To me, that is a declaration to the contrary.

My final question is: Does the administration believe that the President has the authority to unilaterally lift the embargo?

Ms. JACOBSON. Clearly not or he wouldn't have welcomed and encouraged the debate in Congress.

Mr. DESANTIS. Well, but we have been down this road before, because he said he couldn't do things a number of times, and then turns around and does them. So I just think it is important to get this on the record. The statute is very clear about what would have to happen in order to have any type of waiver of these restrictions, and there is no evidence that any of those criteria have been met up to this point. Is that accurate?

Ms. JACOBSON. I am sorry. A waiver of—to have lifting of what kind of restrictions? Of the embargo?

Mr. DESANTIS. Any type of provisions that can be waived requires there are certain provisions that are listed that must occur in order for the President to act.

Ms. JACOBSON. To act to lift the embargo, the President was clear in the State of the Union that he wants that to be debated in Congress.

Ms. ROS-LEHTINEN. Gentleman's time has expired.

Mr. DESANTIS. Yield back.

Ms. ROS-LEHTINEN. Thank you, Mr. DeSantis.

Mr. Castro of Texas.

Mr. CASTRO. Thank you, Chairwoman, and like many of my colleagues, I have been moved by the testimony of Ms. Ros-Lehtinen and also my colleague Albio Sires, who are Cuban American, and many Cuban Americans, particularly of a more senior generation lost their family members, lost property, lost their livelihoods in their country, and for many years I think much of our foreign policy toward Cuba was in great deference to that fact, and when you hear the stories that is very understandable.

I do think with the President's change in normalization in diplomatic relations toward Cuba that the power of American culture and the power of our technology and our democracy will ultimately win out, and I think that in many ways, this was a start of a new revolution in Cuba, and as the Castro brothers are in the winter of their reign, I see this as positioning the United States for when they are gone.

And so with that in mind, let me ask you, how does it position our country vis-à-vis Cuba once these folks are no longer in power?

Ms. JACOBSON. Thank you, Congressman. I think, you know, this really is the question. One of the things that is critical is the next generation of activists, of leaders, we want to keep faith with them. I thought one of the most important things in this policy is how we work with the current human rights activists and democracy leaders, the new entrepreneurs and artists and expand civil society. How do we encourage them when Tania Bruguera wanted to have performance art in Revolutionary Square and asked Cubans to speak openly, 300 artists wrote in support of her effort. Many of them had never made a political statement before. So it is the idea of expanding people's engagement in civil society, which is novel, and is important in preparing for what comes next in Cuba.

Mr. CASTRO. Sure. And I know in places like China, for example, they can't access social media sites, but they have access to the Internet. Many in Cuba have no access even to the Internet. Is that right?

Ms. JACOBSON. Absolutely.

Mr. CASTRO. And also—and I don't know. I got here a little bit late, because like many of my colleagues, I have two committee meetings at the same time, but let me ask you, what becomes of the wet foot/dry foot policy?

Ms. JACOBSON. At this point, Congressman, we have no plans to change that law, and it would—the law, obviously, is in on the books. That would be have to be changed by Congress. We have no plans to request such a change.

Mr. CASTRO. Okay. Thank you.

I yield back, Chairwoman.

Ms. ROS-LEHTINEN. Thank you, Mr. Castro.

Mr. Emmer of Minnesota.

Mr. EMMER. Thank you, Madam Chair, and thank you to the panel.

It is interesting, I hear often in the past few weeks that if something hasn't been working for 50 years, you should look at changing it, but nobody seems to go directly to the issue, except some of the comments I have heard today about how nothing has changed within the country, and I am interested in a couple of things, because much of it has been covered already, but the President broke with policy by appointing a couple of White House aids to conduct these secret negotiations. I am interested, and I think it is probably Ms. Jacobson, because you seem to have at some point been brought in and made aware of what was going on, what happened that caused that moment in time where the President decided to appoint these two to negotiate secretly with the Cubans, and why? Why did he break from policy?

Ms. JACOBSON. I can't—I can't answer that question on behalf of the President.

What I can tell you is that one of the two people engaged in those discussions is a foreign service officer on loan to the White House, a foreign service officer who is one of our foremost experts on Cuba, having served there and on the Cuba issue at the State Department.

Mr. EMMER. But you don't know what suddenly sparked now is the time that this has to happen?

Ms. JACOBSON. I think there has long been a concern within the administration that the policy was not effective in empowering the Cuban people.

Mr. EMMER. So let me ask you this, then, Ms. Jacobson, because many of the questions are—I mean, I heard from Representative Connolly and others, what did we get?

If I understand your testimony today, these secret negotiations included, for instance, discussions about the brutalization of families. In other words, how you are going to compensate these families for their personal loss during the Castro takeover and since, and there has been a promise that that will be part of the negotiations before actual—there will be a proposal to "dismantle the embargo."

Ms. JACOBSON. What has to be part of full normalization of relations, that is, making the relationship with Cuba look like every other normal one, and that is the full range of things, not just diplomatic relations, is a process and a resolution of this longstanding issue of claims, which the Foreign Claims Settlement Commission has, and judgements, yeah.

Mr. EMMER. Got it. All right. So—and I just want it on the record so I understand, because you have separated between diplomacy and complete normalization, which would be lifting the embargo and things that the President says he cannot do as the Executive, only Congress.

Ms. JACOBSON. Right.

Mr. EMMER. When we talk about the diplomacy, opening an Embassy, hopefully getting to travel across the island, which right now has not been assured, that is diplomacy, and these few things that the administration can do without Congressional approval.

The next step, my understanding from your testimony today is, there has been a promise that there will be, as part of any agreement moving forward, any final agreement, an understanding as to how these families will be compensated, not only for their personal loss, but for their property losses. Is that correct?

Ms. JACOBSON. There will be a process with the Cuban Government to come to resolution of those issues.

Mr. EMMER. So you may not require that they be reimbursed or compensated for loss of——

Ms. JACOBSON. I don't—I think in all of these kinds of cases, and I will ask my colleagues if they have any comment, but it may be Department of Justice that would be placed to answer this, in all of these kinds of things, it has to be agreed between—mutually between two countries to resolve those——

Mr. EMMER. I understand, but you led us to believe, at least you led me to believe, that when these discussions were taking place, these are issues that were, in fact, raised and have been discussed, and it would lead me to believe, listening to questions here today, that there are things that are going to be required if Congress is ultimately going to approve a full normalization.

Ms. JACOBSON. Right, and that means a satisfactory resolution, which means we have to be satisfied, but the Cuban Government will have to be satisfied, too, for an agreement.

Mr. EMMER. And that would include this harboring of murderers and thieves and criminals by the Castro regime?

Ms. JACOBSON. The question of fugitives—if you mean the question of fugitives or——

Mr. EMMER. I added it to—you put all of these together today, and I see my time is running out.

My point is that you made it sound as though these are all going to be necessary requirements to a final agreement if it is actually going to be fully normalized, and I believe my time is expired, Madam Chair.

Ms. ROS-LEHTINEN. Thank you so much. Thank you.

Mr. Clawson of Florida.

Mr. CLAWSON. Thank you for coming today.

I would like to ask a question or two about this deal's impacts on religious freedom in Cuba. I represent South Florida, Southwest Florida, and of the, you know, 94 percent of the Jewish folks left after the revolution, some of them came to my district. So this is a question I am sure that is on a lot of their minds of those that remain that are family members. But there is also other religious folks that have been persecuted in Cuba. Christians. We don't talk about Mormons much, but there are two Mormon branches, I understand, in Cuba, and other religious minorities as well. So I am wondering about the impact of this deal on tolerance for religion in general, and will missionaries and other folks from different sects be allowed to go now and help their brothers and sisters on the island?

Ms. JACOBSON. Well, I think—I think it is really important, Congressman. The regulations—and I could let my colleagues—this really expands the ability of religious groups to go, because what

60

we have done is make the religious missions part of this, the religious opportunities general license, and so we are hoping that there are a lot more religious groups that are able to go and see counterparts in Cuba and have that interaction.

In terms of the tolerance for religious freedom in Cuba, I certainly hope that there will be an impact certainly by having their brethren come and work with them and support them.

I visit the Jewish community every time I go to Cuba, and I visited this time with the church, and there was recently, you know, obviously the announcement of a new church to be built, a new Catholic church to be built in Cuba, but it is a very important part of what we are hoping to stimulate as part of civil society.

Mr. SMITH. I could just add to that, that in the past, many Americans had to come to OFAC and seek what is called a specific license to be able to go to Cuba to engage in religious activities, and one of the changes that we made was to authorize that in our regulations, which means that people may now go to Cuba for religious activities or for religious purposes without coming to this government agency to seek approval first.

Mr. BORMAN. And there are two pieces on our side. One is that for those trips that are now generally authorized for religious purposes, the things that the travelers want to bring with them also can be done under a general authorization rather than coming and waiting for a specific authorization from us.

And another piece of our license exception allows building materials to be exported for private sector use, including building of churches, for example, again, without individual licenses under this general authorization.

Mr. CLAWSON. I hope that we will have measurables here. I am always worried about bait and switch and using some other aspect of the law to really get around things that are uncomfortable, and I personally just think it is hard to have a meaningful life for a lot of folks if they don't have a meaningful religious experience. So I am hoping that the administration will follow up here to where we actually see meaningful, opening and meaningful religious awakening on the island for so many that want it.

Ms. JACOBSON. Thank you, sir.

Mr. CLAWSON. I have no more to say. I yield back.

Ms. ROS-LEHTINEN. Thank you, Mr. Clawson.

Mr. Weber of Texas.

Mr. WEBER. Well, thank you, Madam Chair, and, gentlemen, I apologize. You all haven't seemed to be getting a lot of the questions, and so let me just ask you all a couple of quick questions. Are you all going to be okay while I question her?

Mr. BORMAN. Yes, sir.

Mr. SMITH. Yes.

Mr. WEBER. Okay. Thank you very much.

Ms. Jacobson, let me start out by saying I have really appreciated your professionalism and your demeanor and your attitude. You have done a good job, and I appreciate that.

Are the State and Treasury regulations now fully in compliance with the intent of Congress, Ms. Jacobson, when it passed the Trade Sanctions Reform and Export Enforcement Act of 2000?

Ms. JACOBSON. Yes, sir, we believe they are.

Mr. WEBER. You believe that they are?

Going forward, and I understand you said the President wants—he doesn't want the dialogue that is happening in Congress, and I appreciated Joaquin Castro, my colleague over here from Texas' comments earlier about moving forward past the current regime. That was an interesting take, but going forward, will the ag trade, and I have rice farmers in Texas in my district and other producers as well, and five ports. So they are very interested in the trade part of this. Will the trade of ag products be able to be conducted without a lot of input, and some would say interference, from the administration?

Ms. JACOBSON. I think that is a great question, and we know that there is an enormous amount of interest in that. I actually may defer to my colleague on some of this.

Mr. WEBER. They will feel good about that.

Ms. JACOBSON. They will, and it will give me a chance to have a little bit of water. So——

Mr. WEBER. Okay. Yes, Mr. Smith.

Mr. SMITH. Well, we made changes in the current set of regulations that changed the financing terms to what the ag exporters had requested. And so, it should be easier for them to be able to send——

Mr. WEBER. Without a lot of red tape?

Mr. SMITH. Without coming in to OFAC for any requirements.

Mr. WEBER. Okay. Good. Mr. Borman, any input?

Mr. BORMAN. Well, one thing that we were not able to address in our changes were—is the TSRA requirement that there be a license that is no more restrictive than a licensed exception. So that piece stays in place, but that is a—currently a 12-day process.

Mr. WEBER. 12-day process? Okay.

Mr. BORMAN. For somebody who wants to make an ag export, comes in and waits—submits an application to us and gets an answer yes or no in 12 days.

Mr. WEBER. Okay. Well, then other than changing the cash-in-hand rule, what other changes in OFAC, do you know, are in the offing? Anybody?

Mr. SMITH. When you say other than——

Mr. WEBER. That would actually give us potentially new opportunities for ag products in particular.

Mr. SMITH. So the other thing that we did was we allowed U.S. banks to establish correspondent accounts at Cuban banks. And what helped with that and with the ag trade is, right now if you want—an American exporter has to get payment from a Cuban exporter, and then it has to go through a third country and then come to the United States. Now under this rule, they won't. They can pay directly and the payment can be faster and easier and make ag exporters more competitive.

Mr. WEBER. Okay.

Mr. BORMAN. And then—sorry. I am going to take another shot, but I think also the travel general licenses now make it easier for people who want to investigate business opportunities in the ag sector to go to Cuba without coming in and waiting for an OFAC license.

Mr. SMITH. In many of the cases before, exporters would have to come into OFAC to seek what is called a specific license to travel down there. Now, they don't have to for a variety of activities that they would use associated with trade, like the marketing and the export, the delivery, all of that can be done without coming into us to seek that license.

Mr. WEBER. Okay, that is an improvement, and then, Ms. Jacobson, I am going to come back to you. Joaquin asked about the dry foot/wet policy. Tell me what that is.

Ms. JACOBSON. It is—the Cuban Adjustment Act allows that Cuban citizens who arrive on U.S. soil are permitted to adjust their status here and remain, whereas those who may be interdicted by the Coast Guard are—if they have no protection concerns, may be returned.

Mr. WEBER. That is what I figured. Well, that is my questions, and I thank you all for your testimony.

Ms. ROS-LEHTINEN. Thank you very much, Mr. Weber.

We were going to go to a second round of questions for the three of us left in case you wanted to ask another question.

The chair recognizes herself.

The Foreign Claims Commission has found that there are almost 6,000 U.S. claims that are judged to be qualified for compensation by the Castro dictatorship. The adjudicated value of those claims, by adding a 6 percent simple interest, according to this commission, makes the total principal value of American claims to over $8 billion today. I don't think the State Department will enforce Helms-Burton by investigating, trafficking, and confiscated U.S. property, nor enable U.S. property owners to secure compensation for the unauthorized use of property subject to a claim.

Do you think that you will or won't, and I also worry that the administration will use our influence to go even further. We will— will we try to help Cuba get membership into the World Bank? Into the IMF? Into the IDB? Other multilateral development banks? And will we prevent any assistance, any financing, or any other benefit from these institutions until U.S. property claims have been resolved to the satisfaction of American owners?

And, lastly, if you could tell us what are the three conditions according to U.S. law under Helms-Burton for the embargo to be lifted, and I know the President is going to present us legislation to free up the embargo, what of those three conditions have been met that would satisfy the embargo—or justify the embargo being lifted?

So first on the claims on what we are going to do, if we are going to help Cuba get into these organizations, and then the three conditions under Helms-Burton?

Ms. JACOBSON. Let she start out by saying I have been cognizant of the importance of resolution of the claims issues and the judgements from the very beginning of this process. It is very important that those be resolved. The State Department as well as other government agencies, the Justice Department under which the Autonomous Foreign Claims Settlement Commission acted to adjudicate and assign values to those claims. We believe very strongly that that has to be part of future conversations over the next years, however long normalization may take. Those are extremely difficult, obviously, to have with any foreign government as those commissions' dealings have proven, but we intend to pursue that certainly as part of our discussion. I raised that in the very first conversation knowing that we weren't going to talk about it that day deeply, but it must be part of full normalization.

Second, on the international financial institutions, there is obviously very specific language in the law about this. We feel that we are not in a position right now where Cuba is, you know, eligible for membership, certainly, and there are lots of——

Ms. ROS-LEHTINEN. You say right now. Do you foresee that Cuba will be moving in that direction?

Ms. JACOBSON. I think, Madam Chairman, we all hope for the day when there would be logical membership, because it will be a free and open Cuba with an open economic system that would be a logical member, but I don't know exactly at what point. We also hope that at some point in the future, they may ask for help to open their system. They are not right now. So——

Ms. ROS-LEHTINEN. But just as we said that we weren't going to swap spies and we did, even though you—a rose by any other name, but you call it something else, will we be advocating for Cuba's inclusion in these international organizations that would allow it to give it credit to continue to oppose the people?

Ms. JACOBSON. We are not advocating for their membership, but we also want to make sure that at some point in time, it may be useful to have organizations like the IMF, not give them help, but help them open their economy, which is what they do.

Ms. ROS-LEHTINEN. Because we are keeping them—these institutions are keeping them from opening the economy.

Ms. JACOBSON. No, no, no, but they don't necessarily have——

Ms. ROS-LEHTINEN. Let's go to the three conditions under Helms-Burton. What are the three conditions that would allow the lifting of the embargo, and what of those three have been met by the Castro regime?

Ms. JACOBSON. I am sorry. I don't have them in front over me. The three conditions in the legislation?

Ms. ROS-LEHTINEN. Well, I hope that when you are negotiation with the Castro regime you keep in mind U.S. law. U.S. law is the LIBERTAD Act of 1996. The President is calling for the lifting of the embargo. Please go and check that out, because that is U.S. law, and we are hoping that you will abide by that.

Ms. JACOBSON. Absolutely.

Ms. ROS-LEHTINEN. And with that, Mr. Clawson has a follow-up question.

Mr. CLAWSON. I believe that good leadership requires all stakeholders to be taken into account. Companies go off track when they only think about shareholders, and in government, I think it is even more important that we keep all stakeholders take them into account and that they are consulted. This felt like a sad decision to me because it seemed to bypass a normal conversation with all stakeholders with respect to Cuba, stakeholders that live in our country, family members and others that got surprised, as you did as stakeholders that work on the front line, and I kind of want to be on the record on that, because I think when we bypass stakeholders, we make unfair decisions that are narrow in their bandwidth, and this doesn't feel—this decision doesn't feel fair because of the process or lack of process that we went through to get here surprising people that have stakes in the game of Cuba. So I wanted to be on the record on that.

I also think makes your job on the front lines a lot more difficult, and I can't imagine surprising folks that work for me, bypassing them and cutting a deal with somebody that—without them knowing it. It feels like that undercuts your authority in the future, and maybe you see that different, but I just don't know how that is not the case.

So I want to say thank you for hanging in there. I think your jobs just got tougher, not easier, and I want to express my appreciation for you all and the service you do our country, and even in times made more difficult like now by leadership, and then along those lines I want to say thanks for hanging in there today. It is not easy coming up here, and, you know, you get it from both sides in our case. So you seem to have done it with humor and hung in there and kept your, you know, your sense of humor here, and for that, most of all, I express my appreciation to you all for making time for us. Thank you.

Ms. ROS-LEHTINEN. Gentleman yields back, and I request unanimous consent to submit for the record a letter from South Florida State and Local Elected Officials to President Obama to express their profound disappointment over the December 17th announcement, an Agreement for Democracy in Cuba, which is a 10-point roadmap from the people of Cuba toward a real transition to democracy, op eds from the former staff director of this committee, Dr. Yleem Poblete, and questions for the record from Congressman Mario Diaz-Balart. And with that, our committee is adjourned.

[Whereupon, at 12:47 p.m., the committee was adjourned.]

APPENDIX

FULL COMMITTEE HEARING NOTICE
COMMITTEE ON FOREIGN AFFAIRS
U.S. HOUSE OF REPRESENTATIVES
WASHINGTON, DC 20515-6128

Edward R. Royce (R-CA), Chairman

January 28, 2015

TO: MEMBERS OF THE COMMITTEE ON FOREIGN AFFAIRS

You are respectfully requested to attend an OPEN hearing of the Committee on Foreign Affairs, to be held in Room 2172 of the Rayburn House Office Building (and available live on the Committee website at http://www.ForeignAffairs.house.gov):

DATE: Wednesday, February 4, 2015

TIME: 10:00 a.m.

SUBJECT: Cuba: Assessing the Administration's Sudden Shift

WITNESSES: The Honorable Roberta S. Jacobson
Assistant Secretary
Bureau of Western Hemisphere Affairs
U.S. Department of State

Mr. John E. Smith
Deputy Director
Office of Foreign Assets Control
U.S. Department of the Treasury

Mr. Matthew S. Borman
Deputy Assistant Secretary of Commerce for Export Administration
Bureau of Industry and Security
U.S. Department of Commerce

By Direction of the Chairman

67

COMMITTEE ON FOREIGN AFFAIRS
MINUTES OF FULL COMMITTEE HEARING

Day _Wednesday_ Date _02/04/15_ Room _2172_

Starting Time _10:08 a.m._ Ending Time _12:47 p.m._

Recesses _0_ (___to___)(___to___)(___to___)(___to___)(___to___)(___to___)

Presiding Member(s)

Edward R. Royce, Chairman
Rep. Ileana Ros-Lehtinen

Check all of the following that apply:

Open Session ☑
Executive (closed) Session ☐
Televised ☑

Electronically Recorded (taped) ☑
Stenographic Record ☑

TITLE OF HEARING:

Cuba: Assessing the Administration's Sudden Shift

COMMITTEE MEMBERS PRESENT:

See Attached Sheet.

NON-COMMITTEE MEMBERS PRESENT:

Rep. Sheila Jackson Lee

HEARING WITNESSES: Same as meeting notice attached? Yes ☑ No ☐
(If "no", please list below and include title, agency, department, or organization.)

STATEMENTS FOR THE RECORD: _(List any statements submitted for the record.)_

SFR - Connolly
SFR - Barbara Lee

TIME SCHEDULED TO RECONVENE _____
or
TIME ADJOURNED _12:47 p.m._

Jean Marter, Director of Committee Operations

HOUSE COMMITTEE ON FOREIGN AFFAIRS
FULL COMMITTEE HEARING

PRESENT	MEMBER	PRESENT	MEMBER
X	Edward R. Royce, CA	X	Eliot L. Engel, NY
X	Christopher H. Smith, NJ	X	Brad Sherman, CA
X	Ileana Ros-Lehtinen, FL	X	Gregory W. Meeks, NY
X	Dana Rohrabacher, CA	X	Albio Sires, NJ
X	Steve Chabot, OH	X	Gerald E. Connolly, VA
	Joe Wilson, SC	X	Theodore E. Deutch, FL
	Michael T. McCaul, TX	X	Brian Higgins, NY
X	Ted Poe, TX	X	Karen Bass, CA
X	Matt Salmon, AZ		William Keating, MA
	Darrell Issa, CA	X	David Cicilline, RI
	Tom Marino, PA		Alan Grayson, FL
X	Jeff Duncan, SC	X	Ami Bera, CA
X	Mo Brooks, AL	X	Alan S. Lowenthal, CA
	Paul Cook, CA	X	Grace Meng, NY
X	Randy Weber, TX	X	Lois Frankel, FL
X	Scott Perry, PA		Tulsi Gabbard, HI
X	Ron DeSantis, FL	X	Joaquin Castro, TX
X	Mark Meadows, NC	X	Robin Kelly, IL
X	Ted Yoho, FL	X	Brendan Boyle, PA
X	Curt Clawson, FL		
X	Scott, DesJarlais, TN		
X	Reid Ribble, WI		
X	Dave Trott, MI		
X	Lee Zeldin, NY		
X	Tom Emmer, MN		

THE WHITE HOUSE

WASHINGTON

January 30, 2015

The Honorable Edward R. Royce
Chairman
Committee on Foreign Affairs
United States House of Representatives
Washington, DC 20515

Dear Chairman Royce:

I am writing in response to your letter of January 22, 2015 regarding the House
Committee on Foreign Affairs' February 4, 2015 hearing on the Administration's recently
announced changes to U.S. policy towards Cuba. In that letter, you invited a member of the
National Security Council (NSC) staff, Special Assistant to the President and Senior Director for
Western Hemisphere Affairs Ricardo Zuniga, to testify.

We are committed to working with you to make sure that the Committee has relevant
information about the Administration's policy changes in Cuba. As the President announced in
December, these changes will end more than fifty years of stalemate and will begin the process
of normalizing relations between our two countries, creating more opportunities for the
American and Cuban people while continuing to advance American values and principles and
supporting the ability of the Cuban people freely to determine their futures. Shortly after the
announcement, representatives from the Departments of State, Treasury, and Commerce, along
with White House staff, participated in multiple briefings of House and Senate staff, including
the staff of your Committee to explain the proposed diplomatic and economic changes.

I believe that we can work together constructively to address the Committee's interests,
but it has long been the policy of Administrations from both political parties to decline requests
for congressional testimony by White House staff. As a general matter, such requests raise
separation of powers concerns, and these concerns are particularly strong with respect to White
House staff who have advised the President and where the requested testimony could implicate
the President's core constitutional prerogatives.

Your letter notes that representatives of the Departments of State, Treasury and
Commerce have confirmed their attendance and will testify at the Committee's February 4
hearing. These agencies have primary responsibility for implementing the Administration's
policy changes towards Cuba and are in the best position to continue to provide information
relating to their progress.

Sincerely,

W. Neil Eggleston
Counsel to the President

cc: The Honorable Eliot L. Engel, Ranking Member

Insert for the Record
Submitted by the Honorable Edward R. Royce

THE WALL STREET JOURNAL.

OPINION

The U.S.-Cuba Deal Heightens the Spy Threat

In May 2003, 14 Cuban diplomats were expelled by the U.S. for 'unofficial activities'—espionage.

By JASON POBLETE and YLEEM POBLETE

Jan. 12, 2015 6:55 p.m. ET

In addition to freeing three Cuban spies on Dec. 17, President Obama announced additional concessions and sanctions-easing proposals as part of his effort to "normalize" relations with the Castro regime in Cuba. Perhaps most troubling is his administration's desire to upgrade the U.S. and Cuban diplomatic posts to embassy status and restore full recognition to the dictatorship.

Since at least the 1980s, a number of Cuban nationals accredited as "diplomats" at the Cuban Interests Section in Washington, D.C., as well as Cuba's United Nations Mission in New York, have been expelled for "hostile intelligence activities" against the U.S., according to the State Department.

More recent expulsions have been due to "a pattern of unofficial activities deemed harmful to the United States." These continuing pursuits by Cuban agents should provide sufficient reason for any responsible policy maker to refrain from normalizing relations.

In May 2003, 14 Cuban diplomats were declared persona non grata by the State Department and expelled from the U.S. for "unofficial activities," which is diplomatic speak for espionage. One was the first secretary of the Cuban Interests Section, Jose Anselmo Lopez Perera. His wife, Josefina Vidal, also a first secretary and known Cuban intelligence officer, left with her husband. In exchange for her "heroic" exploits on behalf of the Revolution—yes, they still talk this way in Havana—the Castro regime rewarded Vidal by placing her in charge of North American Affairs or the "United States Division" as Cuba's Foreign Ministry refers to it.

In her capacity as chief anti-American operative, Vidal traveled to the U.S. in May 2014 to meet with State Department officials. Her interlocutor? Assistant Secretary of State for Western Hemisphere Affairs Roberta Jacobson, whom President Obama has chosen to lead a high-ranking delegation to Havana this month for normalization talks.

With elevated diplomatic status comes enhanced capacity and flexibility for these regime operatives to engage in hostile activities. The new Congress, specifically the House and Senate committees on foreign affairs, should re-examine this issue, cross-reference and study cases, and assess the president's decision to restore diplomatic ties in context by considering the range of regime activities against U.S. interests.

As Sen. Bob Menendez (D., N.J.), then-chairman of the Senate Foreign Relations Committee, said last month after the release of the three Cuban spies in exchange for Alan Gross, a contractor for the U.S. Agency for International Development jailed in Cuba since 2009: "President Obama's actions have vindicated the brutal behavior of the Cuban government. There is no equivalence between an international aid worker and convicted spies."

When President Dwight Eisenhower officially severed ties with Havana on Jan. 3, 1961, he issued the following statement: "There is a limit to what the United States in self-respect can endure. That limit has now been reached." Havana's communist guerrilla leaders had violated the rights of Americans, directly threatened U.S.

interests, and defied international legal and humanitarian standards. This could not be allowed to continue without a firm response from the U.S. The same is true today, possibly more so.

Has there been a fundamental change in the behavior, policies and actions of the Castro regime in Cuba? No. Has it done anything to merit reversal of the Eisenhower decision? No. (On Monday, news emerged that Havana had finally honored its recent agreement to free 53 individuals whom the U.S. considers political prisoners. But the U.S. appears to have no way of ensuring that their future dissent will not result in imprisonment, as countless others languish in jail for their pro-democracy advocacy.)

Is there a different leadership in Cuba—one that espouses freedom and no longer threatens the U.S. or undermines its interests and objectives? Absolutely not.

Under the Cuban Liberty and Democratic Solidarity Act, signed into law by President Clinton in 1996 and which could be viewed as also codifying the Eisenhower decision to sever ties with Cuba, the legal criteria for normalization of relations, including the political reward of full diplomatic recognition, have clearly not been met.

It is incumbent upon Congress to be the responsible party and focus on U.S. national security and foreign-policy priorities that have been lost in the euphoria over access to Cuban beaches, cigars and rum. It must act swiftly and resolutely—using all statutory, legislative, oversight and funding tools at its disposal.

Only then can the members of the House and Senate hope to prevent the further erosion of American dignity and self-respect that President Eisenhower sought to preserve and that has been damaged by the Obama administration's recent actions.

Mr. Poblete is an attorney and former co-chairman of the National Security Committee of the American Bar Association's Section of International Law. Ms. Poblete is former chief of staff of the House of Representatives' Foreign Affairs Committee and a fellow at The Catholic University of America.

Written Statement for the Record

Alan P. Gross

"Cuba: Assessing the Administration's Sudden Shift"

House Committee on Foreign Affairs

February 4, 2015

Chairman Royce, Ranking Member Engel, and Members of the Committee:

I appreciate the opportunity to submit this brief statement for the record. As the Members of the Committee know, I recently concluded five years of imprisonment in Cuba due to my participation in a USAID-sponsored program authorized and funded pursuant to the Helms-Burton Act. Prior to my incarceration, I spent more than 30 years in 54 countries working to bring about positive change through USAID and other development programs. Much of my work involved increasing the availability of information access to populations around the world. Indeed, this was the fundamental purpose of the project in Cuba for which I ultimately was forced to forfeit five years of my life. I fully support what the President is doing to meaningfully improve international relations, particularly with Cuba. My five years in Cuba did not deter me from wanting to bring about change through development and engagement. To the contrary, I believe more strongly than ever that the President's decisive first steps need to be followed by Congressional action ultimately repealing Helms-Burton and related statutes.

I understand that this hearing is to focus on Cuba and human rights. In my opinion, access to information is itself a fundamental human right and is essential to empowering the Cuban people.

It bears emphasis that all people are decision-makers in various ways, even if their decision is to do nothing. Decisions are made, correctly or not, on knowledge and perceptions derived from *information to which individuals have access.* Access to information enables people to make better-informed decisions and to give informed consent. The accuracy of such decisions depends upon the availability of information, and the quality, timeliness, and cost of access to that information. Based on my experience, the citizens of Cuba could, and likely would, be more decisive if they had better access to information. *Information is food for the brain*; nothing can reach its full capabilities without food. Insufficient access to information is unhealthy for any citizenry and it materially impacts human rights issues on all levels.

If access to information is considered a human right, the Government of Cuba's legalization of access to the Internet in June of 2013 represented a step forward for Cubans in this regard. The Internet, that information highway, is one of the most impactful paths an individual can take in order to obtain and communicate information.

It is probable that the Government of Cuba is finally recognizing that the intellectual and competitive capabilities of its population will be enhanced with less-restrictive practices involving information. It is probable that the Government of Cuba is beginning to understand that Cubans cannot compete in world markets without the same tools that nearly everyone who competes has at his or her disposal, and that Cuba must compete if it is to survive economically.

By easing Internet restrictions, even if ever so slightly, the Cuban Government is beginning to show some new-found respect for the fundamental right of its people to access information, even if the Government does not necessarily like it. Re-establishing diplomatic relations with the Government of Cuba is only a first step in re-establishing freedom of information for those who live on that island. However, it is an essential step. Why would anyone not want to take that step?

Statement for the Record
Submitted by the Honorable Eliot L. Engel
On Behalf of Congresswoman Barbara Lee

Mr. Chair, Ranking Member Engel, and Committee Members:

Thank you for the opportunity to submit my comments and questions for the record on the occasion of this important hearing.

Since the 1970's I've travelled to Cuba more than 20 times and led several Congressional delegations to the island. Each time I've been struck by how much both of our nations would benefit from improved relations.

That is why I applaud the President for his historic step towards normalizing relations with our neighbor. In the more than fifty years since the embargo began, U.S. policy towards Cuba has been an unpopular failure and it is past time for change.

Now the onus is on Congress to act. I was pleased to co-lead the House version of a bipartisan, bicameral bill, H.R. 664, to end the travel ban to Cuba introduced this week by Congressman Mark Sanford. We need to continue this progress by implementing a full repeal of the failed embargo.

I am also pleased that the President's actions resulted in the release of Alan Gross, who has stated for the record to this committee that "My five years in Cuba did not deter me from wanting to bring about change through development and engagement. To the contrary, I believe more strongly than ever that the President's decisive first steps need to be followed by Congressional action ultimately repealing Helms-Burton and related statutes."

In the wake of the President's announcement, much attention has been paid by hardliner adherers to our outdated policies to the state of human rights and democracy in Cuba.

I agree—the wellbeing and rights of the Cuban people are paramount. What I fail to see is how opponents of the President's leadership could interpret the renewal of our diplomatic relationship as somehow undermining our efforts to promote a free and fair Cuban society. In fact the opposite is true—it gives us the opportunity to have these discussions in a direct and open manner, rather than through misguided and disastrous covert operations.

I thank the Chair and Ranking Member for giving us the opportunity to hear this testimony. I would like to turn to several questions:

MATERIAL SUBMITTED FOR THE RECORD BY THE HONORABLE ILEANA ROS-LEHTINEN,
A REPRESENTATIVE IN CONGRESS FROM THE STATE OF FLORIDA

February 3, 2015

The Honorable Barack Obama
President of the United States of America
The White House
1600 Pennsylvania Avenue, N.W.
Washington, D.C. 20500

Dear Mr. President:

As duly elected officials of Cuban-American communities in the State of Florida, we write you to express our profound disappointment over the announcement you made concerning Cuba on December 17, 2014. A day that our communities will not soon forget.

We express our opposition to your administration negotiating without the input of the Cuban people inside or outside of Cuba. Neither Fidel Castro nor Raul Castro are elected by the Cuban people and negotiating with them directly legitimizes their unlawful rule. It sends a message to the world that the United States will conduct business with those who usurp power that belongs to the people. What is more your administration did not consult with those elected officials who represent the Cuban-American communities in the United States.

We express our opposition to the Cuban regime opening any consulates in our communities. Many of our residents are political refugees who left Cuba for fear of persecution by the Cuban regime. We are concerned that an opening of consulates in our communities will expose our residents to great risk. There are countless testimonials of how members of the Cuban Interests Section in Washington, DC have harassed and intimidated congressional staff of Members who have denounced the Cuban regime's human rights record. As noted by former U.S. defense and intelligence official Daniel J. Gallington, "The record of Cuban spies in our country is long and of major concern to our counterintelligence services and agencies. Cuba's spying program will no doubt also be enhanced by the Castro government as it expands its ability to gather national security information against us, both in Cuba and in the United States."

We express our opposition to the release of the convicted Cuban spies who conspired to kill the members of the Brothers to the Rescue. These young men were members of our communities and the pain of their murder is very much real and still palpable. The families of these young men are inconsolable and overcome with grief at your decision to free the men responsible for this heinous crime.

It is our hope that your administration will give our communities' concerns due consideration and reverse your decision to grant the Cuban regime concessions it does not deserve.

Sincerely,

Senator Anitere Flores Chairwoman, Miami-Dade Delegation The Florida Senate	Representative Jose Felix Diaz Vice Chairman, Miami-Dade Delegation, Florida House of Representatives
Representative Frank Artiles Florida House of Representatives	Representative Bryan Avila Florida House of Representatives
Representative Michael Bileca Florida House of Representatives	Representative Manny Diaz, Jr. Florida House of Representatives
Senator Miguel Diaz de la Portilla The Florida Senate	Representative Erik Fresen Florida House of Representatives
Senator Rene Garcia The Florida Senate	Representative Jeanette Nunez Florida House of Representatives
Representative Jose Oliva Florida House of Representatives	Representative Holly Raschein Florida House of Representatives
Representative Carlos Trujillo Florida House of Representatives	Commissioner Esteban Bovo, Jr. Vice-Chair, Miami-Dade Board of County Commissioners
Commissioner Rebeca Sosa Miami-Dade Board of County Commissioners	Mayor James Cason City of Coral Gables
Mayor Jose Diaz City of Sweetwater	Mayor Tomas Regalado City of Miami

MATERIAL SUBMITTED FOR THE RECORD BY THE HONORABLE ILEANA ROS-LEHTINEN,
A REPRESENTATIVE IN CONGRESS FROM THE STATE OF FLORIDA

NATIONAL REVIEW ONLINE

JANUARY 6, 2015
Yes, Cuba Is a State Sponsor of Terror
By Yleem Poblete & Jason I. Poblete

The most senior U.S. delegation in decades will soon be in Havana to engage a declared enemy of the United States in discussions about "normalizing" relations. Covering much more subject matter than routine migration issues, these meetings stem in large measure from the December 17 return of spies to Cuba who are responsible for American deaths.

Obama sent three Cuban spies back to the island, trading them for the release of American Alan Gross. Mr. Gross had been held hostage for five years for the "crime" of teaching Jewish Cubans how to connect to the Internet. As part of this lopsided deal, the Obama administration also declared American policy a failure and offered a large basket of potential economic and diplomatic benefits.

This was a significant ideological and political victory for the Communist regime. And there are more rewards in the offing. Administration officials are reportedly considering removing Cuba from the U.S. list of state sponsors of terrorism — a request Raul Castro made in May 2014 and one that the Cuban regime has made many times in recent years. Under Section 6(j) of the Export Administration Act, a country's designation as supporting acts of international terrorism may be rescinded in only two ways. Cuba is not ready to come off that list. Quite the opposite.

In the first instance, the President must certify to the Congress that there has been a fundamental change in the leadership and policies of the government in question, as was the case with Iraq after the removal of Saddam Hussein. There is no legitimate way that administration officials can make such a claim with respect to Cuba. Moreover, the criteria for determining such a systemic transformation is clearly defined in the LIBERTAD Act, known as the Helms-Burton law. For starters, as stated in the law, Fidel and Raul Castro cannot be part of the governing structure.

That leaves only the second option for removal from the list. To remove Cuba's terrorism designation, the president would need to submit a report to Congress, 45 days prior to the proposed removal, certifying that 1) the regime has not provided any support for international terrorism during the preceding six months and 2) the government has provided assurances that it will not support acts of international terrorism in the future. Most would agree that Cuba fails on both counts.

Cuba has supported and provided safe haven to members of the Basque Fatherland and Liberty (ETA) and the Revolutionary Armed Forces of Colombia (FARC). Both are U.S.-designated Foreign Terrorist Organizations (FTOs). The Obama administration would therefore need to remove ETA and FARC from the FTO list, before removing Cuba from the state-sponsors-of-terrorism list. Both actions are untenable at this time. Unless Spain's foreign-policy establishment is about to make a radical shift in thinking, ETA remains a terrorist organization and there are ETA sympathizers in Cuba who are wanted for terrible crimes against the Spanish people. As for FARC, despite the faux peace process in Havana the past few months, it continues to carry out violent acts in Colombia, has no plans to lay down arms anytime soon, and has links to al-Qaeda in the Lands of the Islamic Maghreb (AQIM).

The "April 2014 State Department Country Reports on Terrorism," however, implied that the only role the Castro regime had with FARC was facilitating travel for the "peace talks" between these terrorists and the

Colombian government. It further stated that the ETA presence in Cuba is diminished. It would appear that a kinder-and-gentler Cuba narrative is being written to accommodate a preconceived policy outcome.

Administration officials have reportedly spent the last two years creating a foundation for Obama's Cuba announcement on December 17 — all the while denying any such activity when asked by Congress about related news reports. If this sounds familiar, it's because it closely parallels the script used in the negotiations leading to the release of five Taliban leaders held at Guantanamo in exchange for Bowe Bergdahl.

The State Department terrorism report also makes references beyond ETA and FARC — most significantly that Cuba harbors several fugitives of U.S. justice. Terrorists, murderers, and other violent criminals are being protected, well fed, and supported by the Communist regime. Among these is a woman convicted of first-degree murder, Joanne Chesimard. Also known as Assata Shakur, she is on the FBI's Most Wanted Terrorists list for executing a New Jersey State Police trooper.
With the help of the Black Liberation Army, she broke out of prison and found refuge in Cuba. According to the FBI, Chesimard "continues to profess her radical anti-U.S. government ideology." New Jersey governor Chris Christie said recently that he wants her back in New Jersey. He'll be waiting a long time.

Basing the decision to remove Cuba from the state-sponsors-of-terrorism list solely on these above-referenced examples (there is probably a great deal more in classified form), the president would need to prove that for the six months prior to the proposed rescission, the Cuban dictatorship did not provide any assistance to terrorists and had unconditionally returned U.S. fugitives. But Communist-party officials have already stated publicly that Cuba considers Chesimard a political asylee and, as such, not to be released into U.S. custody.

The president would also have to accept as credible the "assurances" from the Havana regime that it would not provide support in the future for international terrorism — a difficult task given intelligence gaps highlighted in the State Department's terrorism report. The pertinent section states: "There was no indication that the Cuban government provided weapons or paramilitary training to terrorist groups," but it provides no further data or analysis on these activities. It also fails to address the relationship and cooperation between Cuba and other state sponsors of terrorism such as Iran, or other entities listed on the FTO List.

And then there is the question of intelligence tainted and manipulated by Americans spying for the Cuban regime. One of the most notorious of these traitors, Ana Belen Montes, used her position at the Defense Intelligence Agency to provide Cuban handlers copious amounts of highly sensitive data, including military contingency plans, details of intelligence-gathering efforts, and profiles of a broad spectrum of U.S. officials.

Congress must therefore require a comprehensive appraisal of the range of Cuba's activities against the U.S. and its interests and priorities before the White House can make any decision on whether Cuba will remain on the terrorism list. The review must cover no less than a 20-year period and include a fresh appraisal of all available raw data used in the Clinton-era Pentagon assessment spearheaded by Montes. The review should include detailed intelligence and analysis of unconventional threats and programs that have dual-use application, such as Cuba's biotech capabilities.

The congressional national-security and judiciary committees must be given full access to all files pertaining to the WASP spy network, including data related to the 1996 Brothers to the Rescue shoot-down, as well as damage assessments for all Americans and non-Americans convicted of spying for the Cuban regime.

However, if President Obama chooses to proceed irrespective of the aforementioned conditions and determines that Cuba should be removed from the state-sponsors-of-terrorism list, Congress would have only 45 days from the submission date to evaluate the rescission proposal and act accordingly.

Members of the House and Senate must therefore be proactive in countering the executive action outlined on December 17 and in preventing further damage. Failure to do so would make Congress complicit in the administration's acquiescence to Cuba's Communist regime; it would undermine American interests and reinforce a message of weakness to other enemies of freedom and security.

Yleem Poblete is former chief of staff of the House of Representatives' Foreign Affairs Committee and a fellow at the Catholic University of America. Jason I. Poblete is an attorney in private practice and immediate past co-chairman of the National Security Committee of the ABA Section on International Law as well as a member of the Federalist Society. Both worked on U.S.-Cuba policy-related legislation and policy oversight during their time on the Hill.

THE HILL

January 26, 2015

U.S.-Cuba policy: Myth vs. reality

By Yleem D.S. Poblete and Jason I. Poblete

In announcing the move to "normalize" relations with the Cuban regime, President Obama referred to U.S. policy as an "outdated approach." This claim was reiterated in his State of the Union address, as if repeating it enough would make it true.

A little history and clarification are in order.

President Dwight D. Eisenhower's response to Cuban aggression was prompted by Havana's systematic assault on U.S. interests. One of the early affronts was the unlawful confiscation and nationalization, without compensation, of private property owned by Americans. Today, those certified claims are valued at between $8-$10 billion. While it is seldom mentioned in recent debates, this issue is the foundation on which U.S. law and policy was constructed.

As the regime began to purchase weapons from the Soviet Union and distance itself from the civilized world, there was a proportional increase in foreign policy tools used by Washington to address growing threats and policy challenges.

From missiles pointed at the U.S. and sending agents to Vietnam to torture American POWs at a camp called "The Zoo", to exporting violence, and destabilizing democratic allies, this pariah state has earned every punitive measure imposed by the U.S. Havana helped create and grow the Western Hemisphere drugs for arms network, as documented in numerous official reports. Hostile acts carried out by Havana's spy recruits in the U.S. government are linked to American deaths.

The regime also continues to collaborate with fellow rogues such as Iran. It harbors terrorists, as well as murderers and other dangerous fugitives of U.S. justice. Despite assertions to the contrary, Cuba continues to earn its slot on the state sponsors of terrorism list and that is one of many reasons why the embargo should remain firmly in place.

But the sanctions do not tell the whole story, as they are just one component of a multi-prong U.S. strategy that aims to weaken and isolate the regime, while supporting those struggling to free their island nation from a totalitarian dictatorship.

U.S.-Cuba policy is both punitive, to hold Havana accountable for actions against U.S. interests, and preventive, as it seeks to rein in the regime's dangerous policies. It protects American property rights, as well as the U.S. economy and financial system from the regime's criminal activities. It has been formulated to ensure American taxpayers are not implicitly or explicitly financing terrorism or subsidizing bad investments. U.S.-Cuba policy is also formulated to ensure the U.S. will have a privileged standing and relationship with a future democratically elected Cuban government.

These priorities are again in jeopardy.

Leaders of the Cuban resistance movement, many former prisoners of conscience as Jorge Luis Garcia Perez (Antunez), have called the Obama administration's "normalization" efforts "a betrayal." Antunez, described as the Nelson Mandela of Cuba, and his wife Yris, were present for the State of the Union address, as guests of Speaker John Boehner. They described the Administration's initiatives as benefiting only the regime and creating further roadblocks to freedom.

This is not, however, the first Presidential attempt at rapprochement with the Cuban regime. Under President Carter, for example, sanctions were weakened or allowed to lapse. President Clinton was preparing to go even further when two civilian humanitarian aircraft, piloted by three Americans and a U.S. resident, were shot down by Cuban military jets over international waters. President Clinton was left with no other choice but to sign the *Cuban Liberty and Democratic Solidarity Act*, known as Helms-Burton. This bipartisan law enshrined the multi-track approach and codified existing prohibitions to ensure these could not be unilaterally abrogated through Executive action.

What specific steps can Congress take to stop the Obama administration? These could include but are not limited to:

- Resolutions disapproving of the president's December 17 proposals and subsequent action pursuant to such announcement for potential violations of U.S. laws;
- Adding Cuba matter to other legislative and legal action pertaining to abuse of executive power;
- Cross-committee hearings and investigations with the use of subpoenas, as necessary, for documents, U.S. government officials and those acting as representatives thereof;
- Prohibition on the use of appropriated funds for the implementation of proposals announced on December 17 or related subsequent action, as well as holds on funds for other Administration priorities, until Congressional review and investigations are completed;
- Prohibition on the use of any funds for the U.S. Interests Section in Havana if the status of the mission or its personnel is altered, without expressed Congressional authorization, from that in effect on December 16, 2014.

The 114th Congress must, as Winston Churchill used to say, "never surrender" to totalitarianism.

Yleem D.S. Poblete is a PhD and former chief of staff of the House of Representatives' Foreign Affairs Committee. Jason I. Poblete is an attorney and former co-chairman of the National Security Committee of the American Bar Association's Section of International Law.

NATIONAL REVIEW ONLINE

FEBRUARY 27, 2014
Call Cuba to Account
Obama should implement LIBERTAD as Congress intended.
By Jason Poblete & Yleem Poblete

This week marks the 18th anniversary of the downing of two U.S. civilian planes by the Cuban military over international waters. On February 24, 1996, Cessnas flown by members of the organization Brothers to the Rescue were patrolling north of Havana for Cuban refugees, who risked life and limb at sea in makeshift craft in search of freedom. Cuban fighter pilots in Russian MiGs encircled the planes and attacked. The planes disintegrated. Killed were three Americans: Carlos Costa, Armando Alejandre Jr., and Mario de la Peña, along with U.S. resident Pablo Morales.

The killing of Americans once again brought home the true nature of the Cuban regime. The political repercussions were felt in Washington, D.C. Until then, the Clinton administration had thought, as the Obama administration thinks today, that the U.S. could negotiate with the Cuban government. But facing the political embarrassment of the downed aircraft, Clinton reversed course and signed the Cuban Liberty and Democratic Solidarity Act (LIBERTAD), which had bipartisan support. It was as far as the Clinton administration was willing to go in taking a hard line on Cuba.

Implementation of LIBERTAD, also known as Helms-Burton, was haphazard at best. The air attack was soon forgotten. A mere two years after it, many had turned their focus to easing sanctions and expanding relations with Havana. That effort continued despite the arrest of the Wasp network of Cuban spies in 1998, the expulsions of Cuban "diplomats" for espionage, and the arrests of Defense Intelligence Agency analyst Ana Belén Montes in 2001, and, more recently, of State Department officials Kendall and Gwendolyn Myers for spying for Cuba. These are just the ones we know about.

The trend toward engagement and appeasement of the Cuban dictatorship has worsened under President Obama. His national-security team has eased economic sanctions in several key areas without demanding or securing any concessions whatsoever from Havana. This is backwards. Like Iran and North Korea, Cuba is a regime that calls for a firm hand, not a velvet glove.

In his first inaugural address, President Obama said, "To those who cling to power through corruption and deceit and the silencing of dissent, know that you are on the wrong side of history, but that we will extend a hand if you are willing to unclench your fist." The rhetoric does not match up with the action. The Obama administration has not only given an economic lifeline to this pariah state but also lent it diplomatic legitimacy. The president chose a widely publicized event to make his point and shook dictator Raúl Castro's hand. Meanwhile, back in the island gulag, the crackdown against pro-democracy advocates has intensified; American citizen Alan Gross was taken hostage in December 2009 and is still being held in a Cuban prison.

U.S. law and policy are supposed to isolate the Cuban government economically while supporting the Cuban people. Cuba desperately needs sanctions eased to secure more dollars and access to the global financial system. The U.S. has an opportunity to leverage that need to press for true democratic change and advance U.S. interests. The Helms-Burton law provides a clear roadmap. Easy? No, but not impossible, if the political will exists.

In LIBERTAD, Congress called on the president to fully enforce, through the Departments of State and Justice, existing regulations and deny visas to Cuban nationals who represent or are employees of the Cuban government or of Cuba's Communist party. Unfortunately, such travel continues essentially unfettered. The regime uses both diplomatic and unofficial cover to spy on the United States and make business deals that contravene U.S. law and policy.

LIBERTAD prohibits indirect financing of the Castro regime and bars aid to governments that provide assistance to the Cuban dictatorship or engage in barter-type agreements or non-market-based trade with it. However, many nations that have received U.S. foreign economic aid, whose debt to the U.S. has in some cases been reduced or forgiven, have turned around and from their improved condition provided non-market-based relief and benefits to Havana. Those governments should be held accountable and forced to choose between expanding their relationship with the U.S. or with the pariah regime in Cuba.

Requirements that the president report to Congress concerning the intelligence activities of the Russian Federation in Cuba are also stipulated by LIBERTAD. While the Russians are assumed to have withdrawn from the signals facility at Lourdes, Cuba, in 2002, the Kremlin has been expanding its economic, military, and intelligence ties with its Cold War client state in other ways. Just last summer the Black Sea Fleet's flagship cruiser, the *Moskva*, the Northern Fleet's *Vice Admiral Kulakov* destroyer, and a fuel tanker all docked in Havana, signaling a strengthening of the Russian–Cuban relationship; a Russian warship was reported to have docked in Havana only yesterday. Combined with Moscow's giving safe haven to Edward Snowden, reports that it now wants to return to the Lourdes listening post to enhance its capabilities of eavesdropping on the U.S. make it critical for the Obama administration to revisit the Helms-Burton language about monitoring Russian intelligence activities in Cuba.

The national-security community continues to rely on assessments developed, directed, or influenced by Americans convicted of spying for Havana, but policymakers need updated estimates on the full spectrum of Cuban-regime activities that pose a threat to U.S. security, interests, and allies. All damage assessments relating to the Wasp network, as well as to the Ana Belén Montes and the Myers cases, should be released to the congressional intelligence, foreign-affairs, and defense committees and be available for review by their members. No further Wasp-network spies should be released to Cuba, particularly since the Havana authorities protect fugitives from U.S. justice, including murderers and kidnappers.

The president should work to reverse the fiasco of the U.S.'s agreement to revoke Cuba's suspension from the Organization of American States (OAS) in 2009. He should follow Section 109 of LIBERTAD, which requires the president to instruct the U.S. permanent representative to the OAS to secure support from other member states in urging the Havana regime to allow the immediate and unrestricted deployment of independent human-rights monitors throughout the island and to allow visits by the Inter-American Commission on Human Rights.

Most important, the administration should turn its attention to securing justice for Americans. In multilateral forums, it should pressure Havana to unconditionally release Alan Gross and should obtain immediate INTERPOL Red Notices for the three Cuban air-force officials indicted for the wanton killing of Americans in February 1996. Since these pilots acted under the orders of Fidel and Raúl Castro, the Castro brothers should also be indicted and prosecuted in the U.S. Further actions should be taken under Section 116(B)(3) of LIBERTAD, which urges the president to seek, in the International Court of Justice, indictments for this attack carried out by the Cuban regime and defined as "an act of terrorism" in LIBERTAD. Since Fidel Castro is not the titular head of state, there is no longer an excuse for doing nothing.

Every nation's transition to freedom, rule of law, and democracy is unique. What works in Kiev may or may not work in Caracas or Damascus. For Cuba, the road has been long, and the days ahead are tough. The roadmap that the U.S. has had in place since the late 1990s should be implemented as Congress intended. With respect to the shooting down of Brothers to the Rescue, the president should at least declassify all records relating to the incident. These documents will afford the families of the victims an opportunity to seek justice in international tribunals. They will do what presidents have refused to do: face evil head-on and ensure that the United States is on the right side of history.

— Jason Poblete is an attorney in private practice and co-chair of the National Security Committee of the ABA Section on International Law. Yleem Poblete is former chief of staff of the House of Representatives' Foreign Affairs Committee and a fellow at the Catholic University of America. Both worked on Cuba-policy oversight during their time on the Hill.

Statement for the Record
Submitted by Mr. Connolly of Virginia

The Castro regime is a communist dictatorship that has maintained its stranglehold on Cuba for over five decades through political and economic oppression. While most will agree with this description, there is significant discord with regards to the policy prescription for unraveling the Castro system as we move forward.

On December 17, President Obama announced a far ranging shift in U.S. policy towards Cuba. As part of the new approach, the U.S. will establish diplomatic relations with Cuba, review Cuba's designation as a State Sponsor of Terrorism, and relax various, longstanding commercial and travel restrictions. The new policy is largely unconditional and drastically alters U.S. Cuba policy.

However, significant doubts remain about the extent to which the normalization of relations with Cuba can, in and of itself, bring about reform in the island nation. We must see the fine print in the concessions the U.S. has made as part of this new policy and demand that relaxed restrictions and greater ties to the U.S. be met with commensurate reforms in Cuba.

Without insisting on reciprocity, we squander initial leverage we have to improve political expression, respect for human rights, and religious and press freedoms.

In the case of Cuba, the U.S. has significant leverage to expend. The Cuban economy has languished for half a century and is, to this day, dependent on assistance from other countries. This includes receipt of 100,000 barrels per day of heavily subsidized oil from Venezuela. The Cuban economy stands to benefit from U.S. investment. It stands to gain far more than our economy in the proposed liberalization of trade, tourism, and direct investment.

As we sift through a new approach, the U.S. should not allow itself to become an enabler to an authoritarian regime. The Administration's new Cuba policy has prioritized new telecommunications investments in Cuba as a way to give the Cuban people the resources they need to embrace greater openness. There is certainly a need in Cuba for this kind of investment where the internet penetration rate is 5 percent, as opposed to 84 percent in the U.S. and 32 percent in the rest of the world. While expanded and more effective telecommunications is a laudable goal, without corresponding reforms the new infrastructure could be controlled and coopted by the Castro regime. This is one such scenario where unconditional policy changes can actually do harm to the democracy movement in Cuba.

In adjusting its implementation of the embargo, the Administration will have to navigate myriad statutes that codify restrictions on U.S.-Cuba relations and precondition trade between the U.S. and Cuba. Section 1706(b) of the Cuban Democracy Act of 1992 (PL 102-484) prohibits entry into U.S. ports by any vessel carrying goods or passengers to or from Cuba in which Cuba or a Cuban national has any interest, and the prohibition can be waived only if certain certifications of democratic governance in Cuba are made. Section 102(h) of the Cuban, Liberty and Democratic Solidarity (LIBERTAD) Act of 1996 (PL 104-114) codifies the U.S. economic embargo against Cuba. The President may only terminate the enforcement of this section of the LIBERTAD Act if a transition or democratically elected government is in power in Cuba. Seeing little hope of such a prospect on the horizon, the President has asked Congress to begin to unwind the embargo through legislation as soon as this year.

Congress will not easily disavow the democratic thresholds set in these statutes. My support for the embargo has always been predicated on the fact that it gives the U.S. a carrot and stick to be used on behalf of the Cuban people. The U.S. should not squander this influence. It will be incumbent upon the Administration and the Cuban government to allay Congressional fears. The new U.S.-Cuba policy cannot be allowed to breathe life into a dying regime. Especially, one that has repeatedly used what little strength it can muster to suppress opposition and deprive its people of basic human rights.

Questions for the Record Submitted to
Assistant Secretary Roberta Jacobson by
Representative Edward Royce
House Committee on Foreign Affairs
February 04, 2015

Question 1:

The Foreign Claims Settlement Commission has certified nearly $2 billion in awards for claims arising out of Cuba's "taking" of properties belonging to American nationals without compensating them after Castro came to power in 1959. Taking interest into account, what is the current value of the awards certified by the Foreign Claims Settlement Commission for claims arising out of uncompensated takings by the Castro regime?

Answer:

Claims primarily related to the expropriation of property owned by U.S. nationals and adjudicated by the Foreign Claims Settlement Commission for approximately $1.9 billion could be estimated at over $6 billion, including interest. The claimants have not received any compensation to date.

Question 2:

How is the Administration seeking to negotiate with Cuba to redress the claims? Were the claims raised in the bilateral talks held in Havana recently? What commitments, if any, did Cuba make with respect to their resolution?

Answer:

The Department is committed to pursuing a resolution of claims and firmly believes the re-establishment of diplomatic relations will provide the United States and Cuba the opportunity to engage more effectively on a range of important issues, including claims. During the January talks in Havana with the Cuban government, we proposed, and Cuba agreed, to begin a dialogue on claims in the months following the re-establishment of diplomatic relations and re-opening of our respective embassies.

The discussion of claims will be part of our broader normalization efforts and will take time. As in all claims settlement discussions, there is a range of complex and longstanding issues that need to be considered.

Question for the Record from Rep. Eliot Engel – February 4, 2015 Hearing on "Cuba: Assessing the Administration's Sudden Shift"

Question for John Smith, Deputy Director of the Office of Foreign Assets Control (OFAC)

Mr. Smith, I understand that a large portion of Treasury's resources for sanctions enforcement are devoted to Cuba.

I certainly believe that enforcing existing sanctions on Cuba is crucial. At the same time, I wonder how this affects our efforts to enforce key sanctions in other parts of the world, including in North Korea and Iran.

- What percentage of funding and staffing for sanctions enforcement is dedicated to Cuba? Will the policy changes announced by the President on December 17th reduce the amount of Treasury resources dedicated to sanctions enforcement in Cuba? Or will Treasury need to continue to devote these resources to enforcement in Cuba because of uncertainty by individuals and businesses about the changes?

[Note: No responses were received to the above questions prior to printing.]

Questions for the Record
Submitted by the Honorable Eliot L. Engel
On Behalf of the Honorable Barbara Lee

Question 1:

The first updated regulations from Treasury and Commerce based on the President's announcement have been released. I understand that these regulations will be updated based on need and input from businesses and other stakeholders.

Is there a timeframe available for the next round of regulations? How best can businesses weigh in?

Question 2:

It is commendable that the Administration has raised the caps for remittances to Cuba. I would like to point out however, that disparities in remittances exist between Afro-Cubans and other Cubans, based on historical patterns that made Afro-Cubans less likely to emigrate.

Is the Administration aware of this growing inequality? What steps could be taken to avoid this inequality from seeping into Cuban society?

Question 3:

Under the President's initiatives, I understand that the State Department is currently undergoing a review of Cuba's placement on the list of State-Sponsored Terrorist countries.

Can you provide an update on when we can expect that report to Congress?

Question 4:

As I have said, I am pleased to see the two nations make the move towards renewed diplomatic ties.

Can you walk through the steps that will need to take place to establish a U.S. Embassy in Cuba and a Cuban Embassy in the U.S.?

[Note: No responses were received to the above questions prior to printing.]

**Questions for the Record Submitted to
Assistant Secretary Roberta Jacobson by
Representative Ileana Ros-Lehtinen
House Committee on Foreign Affairs
February 04, 2015**

Question1:

According to numerous press reports, Adriana Perez, a member of the espionage "WASP" network, was artificially inseminated in Cuba while her husband, Gerardo Hernandez, was serving a double life sentence for conspiracy to commit murder and espionage, and had no access to conjugal visits. According to press reports, in an extraordinary concession to a conspirator to murder and espionage, the United States facilitated the artificial insemination.

   a) What was the process at the U.S. Department of State for approving this strange concession to the only person held accountable for the Brothers to the Rescue shoot-down?

   b) How was the transport arranged, which U.S. government agencies were involved, which agency and/or individual transported the sample, and at what cost to U.S. taxpayers? What was the Department of State's role in arranging?

   c) Is there any precedent for the U.S. government, and particularly the U.S. Department of State, facilitating the impregnation of a federal prisoner's spouse? Has any country provided that option to a United States citizen or resident?

   d) Some reports indicate that the United States facilitated Adriana Perez's impregnation as a "goodwill gesture" to gain better treatment for U.S. citizen Alan Gross in prison. If that is the case, what does it say about the Castro regime that the U.S. must provide extraordinary and strange concessions simply to have an innocent prisoner treated humanely? How could that regime possibly deserve normalized relations with the United States?

Answer:
The Cuban government approached the Department of State with a longstanding request to assist Adriana Perez-Oconor conceive a baby with her husband, Gerardo Hernandez. The Department of State facilitated this request as a humanitarian accommodation after consultation with the Department of Justice.

Question2:

Following the January 2015 negotiations in Havana, Assistant Secretary Roberta Jacobson said, "We have ... to overcome more than 50 years of a relationship that was not based on confidence or trust, so there are things we have to discuss before we can establish that relationship and so there will be future conversations" (emphasis added). Now, taking into account the following points:
   • the administration's 18 months of secret negotiations with the Castro dictatorship,
   • President Obama's broken promise made in Miami on May 24, 2008 that he would begin normalization only after steps toward democratization had taken place in Cuba,
   • former deputy national security advisor Tony Blinken assurance in November 2014 that there would be full consultation with Congress before the administration would change policy on Cuba, and
   • the administration's repeated declarations that there was "no equivalency" between Alan Gross and convicted spies,
a. What is this administration doing to repair the lost "confidence or trust" with Congress?

Answer:

 The objective of our Cuba policy has been and continues to be to empower the Cuban people to build a democratic, prosperous, and stable country – a goal we all share. Our previous approach for over a half century, though rooted in the best of intentions, failed to accomplish our objective of empowering Cubans to build an open and democratic country. Our new approach to Cuba gives us greater ability to support the Cuban people and to provide them with the resources and information to freely determine their own future.

 The Administration remains committed to working with Congress to effect this new approach to Cuba. We have remained engaged with Congress on issues related to Cuba policy and value the input and advice from members who represent a diversity of views and interests. Our foreign policy is more effective and sustainable when it benefits from strong Congressional engagement. While President Obama has exercised his executive authority to update and refine our Cuba policy, we also look forward to working with Congress on further needed legislative changes, up to and including the potential lifting of the U.S. embargo. We look forward to working together to promote respect for human rights and fundamental freedoms in Cuba, and support the Cuban people.

Question3:

The 18-month secret negotiations with the Castro dictatorship began in June 2013. The next month, the Cuban dictatorship was caught smuggling 240 tons of weapons - MiG fighters and parts, anti-aircraft missiles, and other military materiel disguised under tons of sugar - to North Korea. A UNSC panel of experts condemned this act as a violation of international sanctions. As a result of this violation, the U.S. Treasury Department sanctioned Ocean Maritime Management Company, Ltd., the Chong Chon Gang Shipping Company and the freighter involved.
Was Cuba's attempted smuggling of weapons to North Korea discussed during the secret negotiations?
Why did the administration sanction North Korean entities but not the Cuban ones that share responsibility for this act?

Answer:

 The United States remains concerned about attempts by North Korea (DPRK) to circumvent international sanctions and strongly condemns Cuba's assistance in the evasion of the UN Security Council's binding sanctions on the DPRK.

 At the same time, the Administration believes that through a policy of engagement with Cuba, we can more effectively stand up for our values and those shared by the international community, promote human rights and fundamental freedoms, and help the Cuban people help themselves.

 With respect to the Chong Chon Gang shipment to the DPRK, this was a violation of UN Security Council sanctions, a multilateral issue. The Administration has worked to ensure that those responsible for this egregious violation of UN sanctions pay a price for their wrongdoing. The United States pushed for the UN DPRK sanctions committee to designate the Ocean Maritime Management Company, a DPRK entity that played a key role in managing the Chong Chon Gang. The committee designated Ocean Maritime Management Company for sanctions last year.

 The Administration worked to maximize the diplomatic cost to Cuba for its role in the incident, including by using meetings of the UN Security Council to repeatedly condemn Cuba's role in the violation. We applauded the UN DPRK Sanctions Committee's release of an Implementation Assistance Notice to publicize the facts of the case. The United States ensured that this Implementation Assistance Notice also highlighted Cuba's role. The international community has unequivocally refuted Cuba's claim that this arms shipment was allowed under UN Security Council resolutions.

Question4:

At the time of the President's Dec. 17 announcement, 14 of those on the list had already been released, some for several months and one for almost a year. At least five of those on the list have already been re-arrested. Since Dec. 17, there have been over 250 political arrests.
How was the President's seemingly arbitrary "list of 53" political prisoners derived and compiled?
Why not demand the release of all political prisoners?
What will be the consequences to the dictatorship for re-arresting some of the political prisoners on the President's list of 53?

Answer:

As President Obama emphasized on December 17, we continue to press for improved human rights conditions in Cuba, consistent with internationally respected norms, and we have no illusions about the intention of the Cuban government to maintain tight political controls. We are constantly monitoring reports of arrests of human rights activists. We want to work closely with Congress on such arrests and in emphasizing the importance of positive changes on human rights in Cuba in general. Neither these 53 individuals, nor other Cubans, should be subjected to harassment, arrest, or violence for simply exercising their rights. We continue to call on the Cuban government to end these practices.

Drawing on lists developed by various independent Cuban civil society groups and international human rights organizations, the Administration provided the Cuban government the names of Cubans jailed for their peaceful political activities or opposition to the Cuban government. The list was not exhaustive nor should the list be seen as the end of our discussion on human rights with the Cuban government. The list focused on people who had been detained for non-violent acts, specifically for exercising their universally accepted rights like freedom of expression.

The Cuban government made the sovereign decision to release 53 prisoners after the two sides concluded and implemented the spy exchange to gain the release of the U.S. intelligence asset jailed in Cuba. A few of the 53 prisoners identified by the U.S. side were slated for earlier release.

Questions for the Record Submitted to
Assistant Secretary Roberta Jacobson by
Representative Paul Cook
House Committee on Foreign Affairs
February 04, 2015

Question1:

Does the Cuban government have basic geographic information using modern technology and software, such as:
- a common set of national map and geographical information at different scales?
- a way to continuously update this information within different organizations of the national and local government?
- a way to share this information within national and local government at all levels?

Answer:
　　Re-establishing diplomatic relations and re-opening embassies will allow us to more effectively pursue our interests and engage the Cuban people on important issues, including this one. Several U.S. agencies have limited contact with Cuban counterparts, some of it under the auspices of the United Nations, on meteorological, hydrological, and seismic issues. However, we are not aware of the full scale of Cuban capabilities or the Cuban government's willingness or technical ability to share geographical information.

Question 2:

Would it be in our national interest to assist Cuba to technically establish such a system, like local, state, and federal governments do in the United States? (This does not necessarily mean we would pay to do so, the question is one of helping Cuba to jumpstart its economy and possible trade with the United States using state-of-the-art commercial geospatial software and technology.)

Answer:
　　Following the re-establishment of diplomatic relations, we will engage in a longer-term discussion of areas of cooperation that are in the U.S. national interest. A full range of issues will need to be considered before we determine which areas to prioritize for future collaboration.

Question 3:

What needs would the U.S. government have for comprehensive and accurate geographic data on Cuba's infrastructure, if our nation's eventually normalized diplomatic and trade relations? Who in the U.S. government would be responsible for this?

94

Answer:
    A comprehensive embargo on trade with Cuba remains in place, although the President called on Congress to begin this year the work of ending it. We have not discussed which U.S. government agency or agencies might need or be responsible for comprehensive geographic data on Cuba's infrastructure.